MW00638970

Ignite CULTURE

Empowering and Leading a Healthy,
High-Performance Organization
from the Inside Out

MARGARET GRAZIANO

Editing, design, and distribution by Bublish, Inc.
Published by KeenAlignment Press

ISBN: 978-1-64704-618-7 (eBook)
ISBN: 978-1-64704-619-4 (paperback)
ISBN: 978-1-64704-620-0 (hardcover)

CONTENTS

TAKE MY
ORGANIZATIONAL CULTURE
ASSESSMENT

This free tool provides speficic, tailored insights to help you analyze the current health of your organizational culture.

visit
keenalignment.scoreapp.com
to learn more

FOREWORD

By Dr. Marshall Goldsmith

As an Executive Coach for more than 40 years, my mission has been to help successful leaders get even better. When my clients come to me with lagging profits, conflict within their teams, or underperformance from the company, it is rarely for lack of talent from themselves or their employees. These are successful people! They're experts in their fields and have hired talented and experienced executives for their teams. The root of their issues most often stems from company culture.

I've found culture to be the most important element for growth, progress, and innovation for a company. Inversely, it is also the biggest reason for lack of employee retention, inefficiencies, and monetary failures. By solving issues around culture for a company, you fix the root of so many issues that hold the team back from achieving their best successes. People work the most effectively, creatively and collaboratively when they feel encouraged and supported by the culture.

I am honored to have had so many incredible clients that inspire me with their demonstrations of humble leadership. One of my great friends, Frances Hesselbein, was the CEO of the Girl Scouts of the USA from 1976 to 1999. On one occasion, I had been on the road for a few weeks with speaking and client engagements, and my last stop was at the Girl Scouts headquarters for a speech with their top executives from around the country as part of an annual meeting.

When I arrived, I was warmly greeted by Frances, and she asked if I needed anything. I told her honestly that I was in need of laundry services to freshen the clothes that had been on the road a little too long. Frances assured me that my clothes would be clean by the morning for my speech, and I assumed they would be taken by a laundry service, so I laid out the things I needed washed in my room and went down for dinner.

I met the heads of the entire Girl Scout leadership downstairs, and we stood chatting for a minute, waiting for Frances to head for dinner. As we were talking, I watched Frances emerge from the hallway—and to my surprise and mortification—she was carrying my load of laundry in her arms. I stood shocked as she passed the group of her leadership team and headed to the laundry services downstairs to drop it off herself before dinner. Although horrified that my dear friend and the CEO of the Girl Scouts was walking my laundry down herself, it perfectly exemplified who Frances was, and what made her leadership so incredible. No task was beneath her—she was someone who jumped in to help, cared deeply for her team, and was always humble and kind. The culture she built was one founded on her actions, rather than words. She never needed to explain how someone should conduct themselves. They all saw her humility on a daily basis.

Ignite Culture is the ultimate guide to becoming the leader and company that inspires others. Creating a culture that uplifts and empowers always starts with *you*. Margaret takes readers first through a journey of self-reflection and encourages them to take an honest look at their behaviors. The second section then moves to a reflection on the team and breaks down the fundamentals of trust and alignment. The third section assesses the organizational health and aligning the company for the mission to create lasting change. This book is the practical and actionable guide to transforming your organization—permanently.

Margaret is an expert in the field of culture change and development. Her work has helped thousands of people across companies heal trust, mend broken relationships, and create space for people to start working together more effectively. Her real stories and experiences combine with research to create an authentic and powerful resource.

This is the book every leader *needs* to read!

Dr. Marshall Goldsmith
Thinkers50 #1 Executive Coach and New York Times bestselling author of *The Earned Life, Triggers,* and *What Got You Here Won't Get You There.*

AUTHOR'S NOTE

They say that adversity is the mother of invention. This has certainly been the case over the course of my professional life. In 2014, I was creating a revolutionary recruiting software when the code was stolen, forcing me to redirect my career. I decided to combine my coaching certification, decade of leading seminars and introductions for large-group self-awareness workshops, and twenty years of executive search and organizational development experience to launch an organizational culture consulting business.

To promote my new venture, I wrote some articles about the importance of healthy corporate cultures and the impact of the leadership team's mindset, behaviors, and overall self-awareness of that culture. The CEO of a company with severe cultural issues read one of my articles and reached out. "We have every problem you mentioned," he told me on a call, "and something tells me I'm the problem." He hired me to run a retreat to bring his leadership team together to solve their many organizational issues. At the time, I wasn't completely sure what I was doing, but I knew I had the right combination of skills to help this team achieve transformation.

Around the same time, I heard world-renowned leadership coach Marshall Goldsmith speak at a Human Synergistics® conference. When he talked about the main theme of his book, *What Got You Here Won't Get You There*, a light bulb went off. The inner work on self is what leaders need most. If they can learn to address their own internal issues, they can learn the authentic human skills needed to lead others and create healthy, high-performance organizational cultures. Inspired, this shaping-culture-from-the-inside-out approach became a hallmark of my coaching and consulting. I began requiring all my clients read Marshall Goldsmith's book and start journaling to see how their mindset, biases, and behaviors might be contributing to the breakdowns in their organizations.

As my coaching expanded to leadership teams, we created two-and-a-half-day workshops to learn how to look inside, own and address personal issues, heal broken relationships, build trust, and start working together more effectively. The feedback was tremendous. The deep internal work, self-reflection, and skill-building around effective communication, respect, honesty, ownership, trust, and authentic empathy helped these groups of leaders tackle the inertia, resistance, and disconnection they were experiencing within their organizations.

A decade later, we've had more than a thousand leaders read *What Got You Here Won't Get You There.* We use the book to grease the wheels and prepare leaders to look in the mirror honestly and open themselves to learning a new way of being and working. Today, the intent of my company, KeenAlignment, is to forever liberate the human spirit at work. And it is my truest honor and joy to watch this happen every day.

Margaret Graziano
Founder and CEO of KeenAlignment®

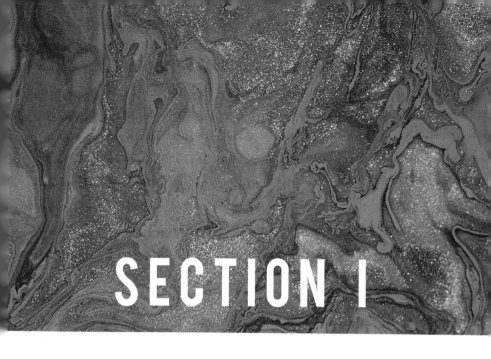

SECTION I

The Leader

Are You the Problem or Solution?

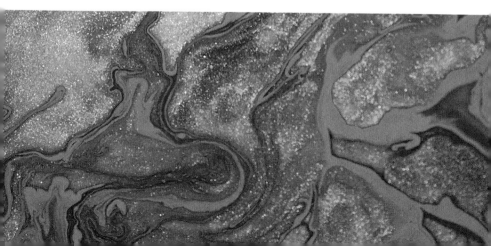

CHAPTER 1

Dysfunction Is Destroying Lives and Companies

"Corporate culture matters. How management chooses to treat its people impacts everything–for better or worse."

—SIMON SINEK—

xcept for the woman in the third row clearing her throat, the crowd gathered on that cold January day was completely still and silent. The group's tired, skeptical eyes were fixated on the auditorium's giant stage, where COO Sam Smith stood in the spotlight looking like a small child wearing an expensive suit. He had been speaking for about twenty minutes, shifting uncomfortably with each revelation.

"I am sorry . . . really sorry . . . for *all* of it." His head dropped, and he stared at the floor. "I have let you all down, and I apologize for that . . . I . . ." His voice cracked. "I . . . didn't know what a jerk I was being. I didn't realize how awful I was treating all of you." Smith took a long, deep breath as the tears began to flow. "I see it now. I know I was making everyone's life miserable. I see what I did to you, and I promise I will do better. We will all do better. This company will do better by all of you. Things are going to be very different from here on out . . ."

The people of C-Corp collectively blinked. Was this really their COO on stage? Could this be the same tough, driven, rude, insensitive boss they'd all kowtowed to for so many years? The man on the stage looked like him, but the words coming out of his mouth were completely foreign. Sam's boss was having a different reaction. His fists and jaw were clenched. His whole body was saying, *What the hell is Sam doing in front of C-Corp's people? Why is he being so damn weak? This is not a company where grown men cry!*

A single person at the back of the auditorium tentatively began clapping, then a few more people. In a matter of a few seconds, hundreds of C-Corp employees were clapping and rising up out of their seats. A muffled "Yeah!" could be heard scattered throughout the crowd of three hundred. Others said, "It's about time!" Such statements grew louder as people patted each other on the back or even hugged. Some were crying. A sense of joy and hope electrified the room. Sam Smith nodded, stroked his hand through his gray hair, and gave a sad smile. "I promise," he whispered with conviction into the microphone. These were the last words he said as he walked off the stage.

The next Monday at C-Corp headquarters, the mood was upbeat and energetic. Sam's speech was the culmination of more than eighteen months of work with C-Corp's team to fix its culture, and the fruits of that labor were finally paying off. Numerous past and future meetings to fix the company's broken, toxic culture were on the calendar. Sensitivity training for the executive team was well underway. A buzz of conversation about change, growth, and a new way of doing things filled the halls. Instead of being tense and stressed, as they had been for years, employees were smiling and showing renewed enthusiasm for their work. A new era was being ushered in at C-Corp.

Employee life began to change. The next two years were creative and productive for the entire company. Sales were up. Profits were up. Retention was at an all-time high. All the key performance gauges indicated something new and positive was happening at C-Corp. The future looked bright. Then, after two years of clear validation of the benefits of a healthy culture, an email from CEO Lance Woodruff hit everyone's inbox: "Due to unforeseen circumstances, COO Sam Smith will be leaving C-Corp, effective April 15. He will be replaced by industry veteran Burt Finch, who brings thirty years of experience to the COO position. Mr. Finch will begin his new role on May 1. Please give him a warm welcome to C-Corp."

Within six months of Sam Smith leaving C-Corp and new COO Finch reinstating the old way of doing things, morale had sunk to an all-time low. Rumors swirled through the halls of C-Corp headquarters about how CEO Woodruff had pushed back when Smith asked him to make important changes. Smith had encouraged Woodruff to do some tough self-assessment and examine whether he was ready to undertake transformative cultural change as the company's leader. Clearly, Woodruff's answer was an emphatic "No!" As a result, Smith was forced out as leader of the change movement. By the end of the first year under new COO Finch, half of C-Corp's executive team had left. Employee engagement had plummeted—and performance along with it. C-Corp would struggle for the next three years.

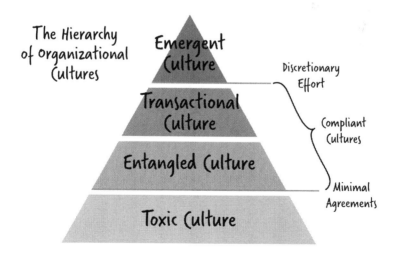

It's this type of dysfunctional behavior that has driven many valuable companies into the ground. Moreover, the problem is so prevalent in corporate America that people are resigning en masse. It has been a key contributor to the Great Resignation. In November 2021, an estimated 4.5 million US workers quit their jobs—an all-time record for a single month, topping other records set earlier in the year. As people reassessed their lives in the middle of a global pandemic—and often handled more work in more stressful conditions—a floodgate of burnout and professional frustration opened. A shocking and widely cited *Harvard Business Review* survey found that "fifty-eight percent of people say they trust strangers more than their own boss"—and this was *before* COVID-19 hit. In the middle of the pandemic, a 2021 survey by Joblist.com of twenty-five thousand job seekers across the US found that "the 'Great Resignation' trend is here to stay. Twenty-two percent of all job seekers report quitting their previous job, and 73 percent of currently employed workers say that they are actively thinking about quitting their jobs." Additionally, the survey found that "workers are unhappy. The Great Resignation reflects a deep dissatisfaction with previous employment situations. Some of the top reasons for workers quitting their jobs this year are unhappiness with how their employer treated them during the pandemic (19 percent), low pay or lack of benefits (17 percent), and lack of work-life balance (13 percent)."

We are living in one of the most volatile, uncertain, complex, and ambiguous times in human history. The world is more connected and moving faster than ever. This means organizations not leading their markets can also fall behind faster than ever. Perhaps this is the wake-up call corporate America needs. Burdened with heavy responsibilities, leaders sometimes fail to recognize that businesses are *human* systems. The revenue, the innovation, the growth—it is all generated by human beings. As President Abraham Lincoln once famously said, "Labor is prior to, and independent of, capital. Capital is only the fruit of the labor and could never have existed if labor had not first existed. Labor is the superior of capital and deserves much the higher consideration." Somewhere along the way, we have forgotten this fundamental truth.

What do busy leaders typically do when things go wrong in the corporate world? Put out the fires. Look for quick fixes. Bring in consultants with fancy new charts, whiteboards, and workflows to "manage" the problem. There are typically some great ideas presented by these consultants. People seem genuinely encouraged afterward. As a leader, you're hopeful that the problem is finally fixed. Often, things do change for a while, but the changes almost never stick. Why is that? Why doesn't anything seem to fix the problem for good? Because this approach addresses the symptoms, not the underlying issue, which is a broken culture. *Companies are human systems that need to be fixed from the inside out.* You can't change a human system without understanding what's driving and shaping the behaviors at every level in that system. You can't put a bandage on a broken culture. You have to find out why people feel broken. It's only after the human system has been healed from within that strategies and tactics can move that human system forward. What I'm proposing is a fundamentally different approach to creating a sustainable, high-performance organizational culture. It starts by igniting the human spirit at work, from the inside out, one human at a time.

The massive dysfunction exhibited daily in companies across America is something few leaders are brave enough to address. The important work that is necessary to create a healthy, sustainable, people-centric, high-performance culture can be daunting. If you are the person in charge of fixing the mess at your company, the road ahead is tough—but don't give up. As someone who has spent the last twenty years working with hundreds of CEOs and leadership teams, I've helped facilitate real cultural transformation—so I know it's possible. In reality, you don't really have a choice. This work *must* be done. A healthy, human-centric culture is no longer a luxury; it's an absolute requirement for any company seeking high-growth or breakthrough performance. It is the key to unlocking the potential of your people, who are the foundation of your company's success.

Still skeptical? Take a look at this chart.

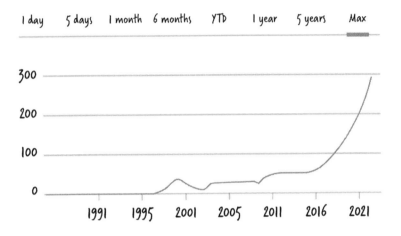

Microsoft Corporation
NASDAQ: MSFT

308.68 USD + 308.43 (3,084,300.00%) ↑ all time

| 1 day | 5 days | 1 month | 6 months | YTD | 1 year | 5 years | Max |

What force of nature was able to push Microsoft's stock price from $50 to over $300 in only five years? What kickass leader grew Microsoft from $88.08 billion in revenue in 2014 to $198.27 billion in 2021? His name is Satya Nadella, the third CEO of Microsoft, and his secret weapon is cultural transformation. His top tools? Empathy, collaboration, and a growth mindset. He has masterfully shaped Microsoft into a powerful ecosystem of continual growth and learning. Microsoft is a stellar example of what a high-performance organizational culture can achieve when a CEO and leadership team commit to cultural transformation. Let's not forget Nadella stepped into his role when Microsoft was described as stagnant, cutthroat, aggressive, bureaucratic, and in decline. Today, Microsoft is cited as one of the most impressive comeback stories on the planet—and its secret weapon is its amazing organizational culture.

You don't have to be running a company the size of Microsoft to benefit from the roadmap Nadella has created. At my company, we work with leadership teams at growing and midsize companies to turn things around or take growth to the next level. And what we've found by working with hundreds of companies across the country is this: transforming an organization's culture sparks a 35 percent increase in employee performance and a 200 percent increase in revenue growth. In other words, mastering the so-called "soft" skills of cultural transformation can translate into a key competitive differentiator and growth engine. Businesses that build healthy, human-centric organizational cultures outperform businesses that don't by a whopping 202 percent. And, when an organization's people treat one another and their customers in alignment with a clearly defined set of core values and a compelling purpose, they perform 146 times better than their counterparts in organizations without stated values or a compelling purpose. It's the secret sauce of a high-performance organization.

Of course, none of this is achieved by paying lip service to culture or if the leadership team is content with slapping a bandage on a status quo that is clearly holding your company back. If the CEO or leadership team refuses to address the dysfunction and toxic behaviors stifling human potential, then the future is bleak indeed—that was true before the pandemic and has become crystal clear since. Buy-in from the *entire* leadership team is required. There must be commitment to the challenging personal and organizational introspection and tough, often emotional, work required to bring about intentional change. If that can't happen at your company, read no further. This book isn't for you.

But what's at stake if you don't start transforming your organization's unhealthy culture? You're gambling, and the stakes are *very* high. Companies with unhealthy or toxic cultures have:

- Declining customer satisfaction
- Higher employee turnover

- Lower growth rates
- Stymied innovation
- Higher absentee rates
- Botched projects and trouble hitting basic KPIs
- Often disastrous decision making
- Bad public reputations
- Trouble finding top talent

Let's look at a real-life example. In 2015, the resignation of CEO Martin Winterkorn of the Volkswagen Group was a very public, international event. It happened just five days after American regulators charged Volkswagen with deliberately falsifying emissions tests for their diesel cars. The company's stocks plummeted, and it took about five years for the company's reputation and stock prices to recover. One might say, "Well, this bad behavior isn't the CEO's fault. It was just poor judgement by some department head." And there you would be wrong. In June of 2021, news broke that Winterkorn would reimburse Volkswagen for $13.7 million. As the *New York Times* reported at the time, "The announcement came the same day that prosecutors in Berlin charged Mr. Winterkorn with lying to the German parliament about his knowledge of the carmaker's emissions scandal, raising fresh questions about his role in a cover-up. . . . The scandal has cost Volkswagen tens of billions of euros in fines, settlements and legal fees."

Cultural dysfunction always starts or ends with the leadership team. Volkswagen is one of many precautionary tales. As discussed in a January 2020 article in *Forbes* called "Crippling Cultures Can Kill Companies," there is a new culture war at hand, and it's not societal; it's corporate:

> When there is a conflict between strategy and culture, culture wins. Just look at Kraft Heinz or Boeing. . . .

Uber is an organization with a need to right a crippling culture Axios.com explains that regardless of the Herculean efforts of CEO Dara Khosrowshahi, there is a lot of the Travis-Kalanick-culture remaining. McDonald's default CEO is also focusing on culture change. *Business Insider* reports that he is engaged in a push to jettison the McDonald's bro-party culture.

Some new CEOs attend to culture change by claiming the Phoenix-syndrome: Although little may have really changed, the claim is that the company is "new" even though the majority of executives are the same, functioning in their same roles. General Motors made this claim, as did the burned-out shell of Sears.

The corporate battlefield is strewn with bodies of unhealthy and toxic cultures. If you don't want your company to become a statistic, it's time to wake up and start healing your broken human systems from the inside out. I'm never going to lie to you about the road ahead. There are no quick, easy fixes in this book. But committing to deep, transformational change will be worth the effort. Once you ignite your culture from the inside out, there are no limits to what the amazing humans in your company can achieve.

Are you in?

CHAPTER 2

Time for a Hard Look in the Mirror

*"The first principle is that you must not fool yourself—
and you are the easiest person to fool."*

NOBLE-PRIZE-WINNING
—PHYSICIST RICHARD FEYNMAN—

What kind of leader are you? Are you someone who shows up in times of wins, both large and small? Someone who shows up in times of failure or mistakes? Someone who shows up when people disagree with your perspective? Do you inspire people with possibility or bog them down with endless tasks?

Since cultural transformation always starts with an organization's top leadership, these are some of the questions I ask senior leaders when we start working together. The most powerful vehicle for breakthrough performance is the people who run the company. In fact, organizational change isn't possible without their commitment and leadership. We saw that happen in the opening story about C-Corp. If your company is struggling or having trouble breaking through to the next level, it's time to take a hard look in the mirror. Are you part of the problem or the solution? Are you ready to commit to authentic personal growth in order to model positive change for your leadership team and people? If you're not, this book will be of limited use to you. I wish you the best of luck. Perhaps we'll meet again. If, however, you're open to a new approach to cultural transformation, please read on.

That's Not the Real Problem

The obstacles holding back your company aren't what you think. The reasons your last company-wide initiative didn't meet expectations are different than you imagine. And the feedback you're receiving about why things aren't working might not be as useful as you believe it to be. There are numerous reasons for this disconnection, but all of them point back to the overall health of your organization's culture. And, in reality, the health of your organization's culture starts with you. Nothing about that statement is meant to judge or question. It's only a wake-up call to start looking at problems differently—from the inside out. This might not be what you're used to hearing, but it's the only way to create significant, sustainable change. This inside-out exploration of your culture's strengths and weaknesses starts with you and the unique power and potential you hold as CEO.

In this book, we're going to explore the underpinnings of a healthy, high-performance culture. One of them is trust. So, as we start this journey together, I am going to ask you to trust me. Rely on my many years of experience building healthy, high-performance organizations and rebuilding broken cultures and then taking them to a whole new level. The first thing I ask you to do is carve out some time for self-reflection as well as personal and professional growth. I understand your time is valuable, so I don't make this request lightly. I just know this is how cultural transformation begins, and it's always at the top levels of leadership.

I could share hundreds of stories demonstrating the difference between how corporate leaders *view* a problem and the *actual* problem.

However, I think the following story that I read in *Forbes* does a great job of making the point. The article was titled "Culture Change: It Starts at the Top" and was written by Grant Freeland, a Boston-based consultant:

> I was working with a major industrial good company a couple of years ago whose CEO decided the company needed to become more customer focused. This, he told me, had become his top priority. But despite letting the company's employees know that "Customers Are No. 1," he wasn't seeing evidence of that. He wanted my advice.
>
> Rather than give him a lecture or a pep talk, I made a request; I asked to see the twelve most recent executive committee meeting agendas.
>
> He didn't understand why I wanted them, but he asked his assistant to make copies for me anyway. Not surprisingly, there was time built in to discuss Finance, Budget, Sales, Quality, Safety, Legal Matters, and other standard fare. Customers were never mentioned. Not once.
>
> How can you expect your organization to be customer-oriented when the leadership isn't customer-oriented, I asked?
>
> He had no answer, of course, and was even, I think, slightly embarrassed. But it was an "aha" moment. He understood—and placed "Customers" on the top of the next meeting's agenda.

This CEO isn't a bad person; he simply suffers from unconscious incompetence—a term used in training psychology that means an individual doesn't understand something and doesn't recognize the deficit. When leaders commit to learning and growing, they learn to admit that they don't know everything and recognize their own unconscious incompetence. This requires self-awareness. In the above case, the CEO had no clue that he was causing the problem. Clearly, no one in his company had told him that he wasn't leading on the customer-centric issue. Not even his leadership team had the awareness or the guts to tell him. That's a clear symptom of a culture problem.

This CEO was looking elsewhere for blame when he should've been looking inward. It's a very common problem, so let's get back to the mirror. According to research, most people believe they are self-aware, but only 10–15 percent actually are. When you look in the mirror, do you see a self-aware person? Take a close look, because there are actually two types of self-awareness: internal, which is how clearly you see your own strengths, weaknesses, values, reactions, and impact on others, and external, which is understanding how other people see you. In *Harvard Business Review*'s 2018 "Emotional Intelligence" series, organizational psychologist and researcher Tasha Eurich summed it up nicely: "Self-awareness isn't one truth. It's a delicate balance of two distinct, even competing viewpoints."

"The first principle is that you must not fool yourself – and you are the easiest person to fool."

Noble Prize winning Physicist, Richard Feynman

Self-Awareness Is a Meta-Skill

Do you possess both external and internal self-awareness? Don't worry if you don't; you're in good company. As the above statistics indicate, true self-awareness is rare. The good news is that self-awareness can be learned. And, if you want to bring about powerful change at your company, self-awareness is a must. In Eurich's book *Insight*, she calls self-awareness the "meta-skill of the twenty-first century" and cites plenty of research about the strong correlation between a leader's level of self-awareness and the company's performance. Self-awareness is no longer a soft skill that you work on at a corporate retreat once a year. It's essential for all leaders. It must be learned, honed, and practiced daily if you want to achieve breakthrough performance at your company. As Albert Einstein once said so eloquently, "We can't solve problems by using the same kind of thinking we used when we created them." So, let's do some new thinking. Back to the mirror . . .

You are successful. You are accomplished. But you have a lot on your plate, and it's lonely at the top. You carry a lot of weight on your shoulders, even on the best of days. What about when things aren't going according to plan? How does that extra weight make you feel? Do you get anxious? Stressed? Angry? What thoughts pop into your head when you feel this way? Do you experience physical sensations as a result of these thoughts and feelings—like sweating or the tightening of certain muscles? How do you act toward others when you are under this sort of pressure? If you can start to answer these questions specifically and honestly, you're on your way to becoming more self-aware. You might even begin to see patterns of behavior in certain circumstances. How do you feel when you have a thought like this: "We're not going to meet our revenue numbers this month. This makes me look bad"? Does your heart rate go up and trigger a reaction—or more likely an overreaction—to the next person who shares bad news with you? Do you start calling all your department heads and questioning them or yelling about their role in the fiasco? Do you think, "Who is to blame for this?" You see, when we're stressed, the amygdala—the part of the brain that helps us process and react to strong emotions—sends out chemicals that narrow our perspective and puts our ego in charge. This is a protective measure that nature has provided through evolution to keep us from harm. But sometimes the amygdala takes over in the wrong circumstances. There's even a name for it. It's called an amygdala hijack. This is when the amygdala reacts too strongly and we have illogical or irrational, overreactive behaviors. If you're a leader, learning how to recover quickly from amygdala hijacks is important. Better yet, do the work necessary to avoid them altogether, and this can become your superpower. Becoming more aware of your thoughts and behavior patterns can help you respond in a more rational and measured way. It's an important step on the road to internal self-awareness.

World-renowned executive coach Marshall Goldsmith, author of the bestselling book *What Got You Here Won't Get You There*, offers a simple and clear gateway to the other side of self-awareness—the external side. He says to simply put your ego on a shelf and admit that you need help, because *everyone* needs help, and *everyone* has blind spots. One of Goldsmith's important leadership rituals is daily questions. In his effort to continually hone his self-awareness skills, Goldsmith has a set of questions that he has to answer every day. They are personal and unique to his own weaknesses. Some are practical, like "Did I exercise for twenty minutes today?" Others are more abstract, like "Did I do my best to find meaning in my work today?" The point is he must answer these questions every day. But he'll be the first one to tell you he isn't disciplined or brave enough to ask himself these daily questions, so he has someone call him every day to ask them and keep him honest and on track. Goldsmith also runs weekly groups for top-tier leaders to help them with accountability in a nonjudgmental environment. This is what the practice of self-awareness and personal growth looks like on a daily basis. Personal growth is a daily and lifelong journey.

21st Century Leadership Competencies

At no other time in recent history has the work world changed so dramatically. The global pandemic reset people's priorities and expectations about their jobs. Navigating such seismic change requires strong leadership. But, according to research, only 18 percent of leaders have the skills they need to do this. What are the skills that a twenty-first-century leader needs to be effective and successful?

- Emotional intelligence
- Communication intelligence
- A focus on goal achievement
- Neuroplasticity and a growth mindset
- The belief that every human has the power to change their behavior (if they want it bad enough)
- The ability to inspire others
- The desire and ability to develop people
- Accountability
- Integrity
- The ability to hire for high performance
- The capacity to build and lead high-performance teams

It's easy to say, "Not a problem. I've got all this." But the reality is that most leaders have a few of these skills but need training and experience to develop them all—and they're all crucial skills to have in today's multi generational and exceedingly distributed work culture. We all have our blind spots. It takes deep self-awareness to look in the mirror and candidly admit our weaknesses. But it's crucial if you want to reach your full potential and lead a high-performance company. You must be what you want to see in your company.

Your Brain Needs to Grow up

As humans, our brains are pretty much programmed by the time we turn thirty. That programming is guided by our reactions to all kinds of childhood experiences—negative, positive, intellectual, spiritual, emotional, and so on. Chances are that, unless you've done the type of work we're exploring here in the pages of *Ignite Culture*, you're probably running your business with your childhood or teenage brain—and that's not good. You might have come up with a number of successful coping mechanisms—many highly successful people do. But, when the going gets rough, these coping skills often don't work. Our childhood brain can show up at work in all sorts of ways, causing us to do things like seek constant validation from others to mask our insecurities or stay extremely busy so that we don't have to face our fears or see the world through a pessimistic lens—like Eeyore in *Winnie the Pooh*, who famously said, "The sky has finally fallen. Always knew it would." That's the type of message the childhood brain tells you when you're reacting to a trigger. It might be a quick way for your childhood brain to make sense of the world, but it's misguided and not to be trusted. You're thinking and behaving based on a set of perceptions that aren't tied to current reality. This is how disconnects happen. Since building and leading a high-performance organizational culture isn't child's play, honesty and self-awareness are required. Once you understand what is driving your thoughts and behaviors, you'll be in a much stronger place to lead others to new heights. The good news is that, if you're willing to do the work, you can override your brain's autopilot and change your behaviors. This is a necessary skill for a highly effective leader, one who has the capacity to inspire people and steer them toward positive change.

Tom was a talented quality engineer who came to me perplexed. He had many strong leadership qualities and couldn't understand why he was completely despised by almost everyone at his company. In his mind, he was doing his job well if he spent the day telling people what they were doing wrong so they could fix it and produce a higher-quality product. He was proud of the work he was doing. Others saw Tom's behavior differently. They described him as "negative," "pompous," and "arrogant." They avoided him and made fun of him behind his back. He couldn't make headway with anyone. I remember the day I walked through the plant with him. People turned away.

Through our work together, Tom began to realize that he could only see what was broken when he spoke to people. He had never learned how to communicate in a way that empowered others. He didn't realize that everyone he spoke with felt he was shaming and blaming them. He couldn't see any of this; it was a massive blind spot. At this point, I had been coaching him for six months. With time, training, and practice, he began to become more self-aware both internally and externally, learning more and more about the disconnect between how he perceived his behavior and how others saw him. He realized the two perspectives were polar opposites.

Within six months of finishing our 18-month engagement, Tom was promoted to plant manager. Two years later, he was promoted again. This time to director of operations for five plants. When he communicates with others now, Tom finds out what matters to the person. He patiently works with them and gets their buy-in so that they're invested in the process of improvement and the outcome. During Tom's leadership tenure, profitability went up eight points, net profits nearly tripled, and the company went from being weeks away from a union walkout to widespread collaboration across teams and operations. The leadership team actually started meeting and working productively together. They engaged in leadership training and organizational culture development with us. They developed a cadence of regular communication. They held town-hall meetings. They had four hundred people go through our Response Agility Training™, where they learned their automatic reactions are de-railing their happiness and causing them undue stress every day. Additionally, we partnered with them to create role alignment for every unique role in the company. It was an amazing turnaround that started with one person being brave enough to look in the mirror and do the personal work needed to create positive change.

Tom is living proof that every human has the capacity to become more self-aware and change his or her behavior. When you start to see such transformations happen throughout a company's human system, the sky is the limit.

KEY TAKEAWAYS

- Building and leading a high-performance organizational culture isn't child's play. Honesty and self-awareness are a leadership requirement.
- As Marshall Goldsmith says, everyone needs help, and everyone has blind spots.
- Every human has the capacity to become more self-aware and get response-able for their automatic reactions that cause stress and has the power to change his or her behavior.

BRAINHACK

A good practice for self-awareness is a quick five-minute meditation that you can do anywhere. Put your feet flat on the ground and take some deep breaths. Focus on one point or close your eyes. Observe what comes up and name everything as either a thought or a feeling. Then name the emotion attached to it. Doing so will activate your medial prefrontal cortex, anterior cingulate cortex, and insular cortex. These three parts of the brain all play a role in the way you perceive yourself. The more often you activate them, the more active they will remain, and the more self-aware you will become.

POWERFUL QUESTIONS

- What is resonating for you in this chapter?
- After reading this chapter, what are the questions you are resisting answering?
- What might be a core challenge in how you lead?

CHAPTER 3

Wake Up and Meet Your Higher Self

"Know thyself."

— PLATO —

Psychologist Abraham Maslow introduced his now famous hierarchy of needs in a 1943 paper called "A Theory of Human Motivation." At the time, his suggestion that people are motivated to fulfill basic needs before moving to more advanced needs was a revelation. Today, Maslow's ideas are widely accepted and increasingly applied in organizational psychology.

The hierarchy has five levels. The lowest level addresses basic physiological human needs like air, food, and water. Next, our species pursues safety, then love and belonging, and then esteem. The highest level of Maslow's hierarchy is self-actualization, which is defined as the complete realization of one's potential and the full development of one's abilities and appreciation for life. Since achieving self-actualization requires us to satisfy all the lower-level needs first, most people never achieve it. In fact, Maslow wrote in his 1968 book *Towards a Psychology of Being* that self-actualization happens in less than 1 percent of the adult population.

In Marshall Goldsmith's latest book, *The Earned Life*, this master leadership coach explores how people maximize fulfillment and minimize regret in order to experience what he calls an "earned life," which he describes as follows:

> *We are living an earned life when the choices, risks, and effort we make in each moment align with an overarching purpose in our lives, regardless of the eventual outcome.*

The pesky phrase in that definition is the last one, "regardless of the eventual outcome." It goes against much of what we're taught about goal achievement—setting a target, working hard, earning our reward—in modern society.

Self-Actualized People

Abraham Maslow, who created the famous hierarchy-of-needs model, wrote in his book *Motivation and Personality* that self-actualization is the "full use and exploitation of talents, capacities, etc. Such people seem to be fulfilling themselves and to be doing the best that they are capable of doing." Self-actualized people, he also wrote, "customarily have some mission in life, some task to fulfill, some problem outside themselves which enlists much of their energies."

High-performance organizations create a work environment and culture that encourages people to self-actualize. But what does that look like in the real world? Let's look at a few famous people in history Maslow felt demonstrated self-actualization. A 2019 article on the "Big Think" blog entitled "9 Self-Actualized Historical Figures" described how Maslow studied a number of historical figures, friends, colleagues, and students to develop his model. Among those whom Maslow felt had achieved self-actualization were President Abraham Lincoln, scientist Albert Einstein, First

Lady Eleanor Roosevelt, feminist Jane Addams, and philosopher Baruch Spinoza. Eleanor Roosevelt, for example, "best exemplified the quality that Maslow called Gemeinshaftsgefuhl, a kind of psychologically healthy social connectedness and concern for other's well-being," according to the article. Among her many contributions to the world, she oversaw the drafting of the Universal Declaration of Human Rights.

All of the self-actualized historical figures Maslow studied were high achievers. If any one of them had not walked the Earth, it would be a different place, perhaps a lesser place, so significant were their contributions to society. Consider an organizational culture headed by a self-actualized leader, one capable of inspiring and encouraging its people to self-actualize—to reach their full potential as these historical figures did. Think about the human potential that would be unleashed in such an environment. Imagine the possibilities in such an organization.

What might happen if you worked toward becoming part of the 1 percent described by Maslow but did so as Goldsmith suggests, without regretting the past or worrying about future outcomes? What if self-actualization for you and your people wasn't a goal but rather an ongoing journey? Could the *process* of working toward self-actualization help you become a better leader? Would this, in turn, have a positive impact on your life as well as your company's people, culture, and performance? You know the answer. You don't have to be perfect to lead others; you simply have to be walking down the right path. Now, think about what this process of change might look like at scale. Imagine the unstoppable energy that you, your executive team, and your people could create if you embarked on this journey together. The upside is tremendous. So, why do so few companies prioritize this valuable and important human work? Because change is uncomfortable. As humans, we are wired by evolution to fear the unknown—so we resist, either consciously or unconsciously.

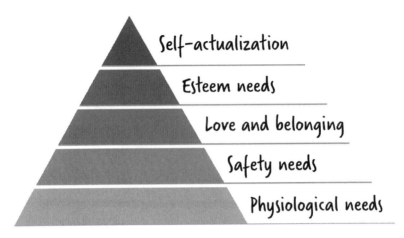

Fear = Resistance

I see this equation frequently in my work. Most of the time, leaders come to me when they're facing big challenges or roadblocks. They're stuck and unable to break through. I'm there to guide them from where they are to where they want to be—to help them get unstuck and transform their companies into high-performance organizations. Most know that our engagement will require commitment and work. My team and I are there to be their partner. We're on the same side. That's why I'm always surprised when some leaders walk into our sessions armed for battle like I'm the enemy. Why? Fear. It's normal. It's our default response as humans. I get it, but fear equals resistance, so we have to build trust and learn how to override our knee-jerk, autopilot reactions. It takes practice, and it's definitely achievable.

Some fear loss of control. Others are afraid to take a hard look in the mirror. Still others feel frustration, anger, or hopelessness. They struggle to shake the negative worldview and practices that led them to our meeting in the first place. Deep down, many are simply worried about having what it takes to achieve personal and organizational transformation. They aren't sure they're up to the task and fear failure and loss of face. *At least right now, I have command and control*, they tell themselves. So strong is the negativity that they would rather ignore that things aren't working and that their company is headed for trouble than submit to the vulnerability required for meaningful change. This isn't a judgement; it's just a statement about how most of us live due to the power of our wiring and years of reinforced behaviors. We hold tight to what we know—even amid decline or imminent collapse—because it *feels* safer, even though it's not.

Let me ask you this: if you were riding on a speeding train across the country for several days—confident you would get to your final destination—and the conductor announced, "The bridge ahead has collapsed," would it make any sense at all to stay on that train? The answer is obvious, but I can't tell you how many times I've encountered fear so strong that a leader would rather ignore the train wreck ahead than change course or get off the train. *The train has gotten us this far,* they rationalize, *and it's what I know.*

Before we can bring our higher selves to work, we need to confront our fears and the defensive, reactive mindset and behaviors that fear creates. This means managing our egos. From an evolutionary standpoint, part of a healthy ego's job is to protect us from real-world threats—thus the fear. Our ego, for example, oversees our fight-or-flight response. This helps us react quickly in dangerous situations. If our brain senses danger, it triggers physical changes to our body chemistry in order to prepare us to flee or stay and defend ourselves. Think of a caveman facing a saber-toothed tiger. We wouldn't have survived as a species if it weren't for our fight-or-flight instinct. But sometimes the ego goes into overdrive. It obsesses over *imagined* threats. It can even cause us to shape events or people into threats when in fact they are not. "The ego does not want an end to its 'problems' because they are part of its identity," bestselling author and speaker Eckhart Tolle once wrote. "It gives definition to our self-image, makes us into someone, and that is all that matters to the ego." When the ego is in overdrive, self-limiting thoughts and behaviors make meaningful growth and change almost impossible.

Plot twist: for those who think keeping things as they are guarantees continued control, it doesn't. You've simply left your ego in charge. Here are a few signs that this might be the case: you always have to be right, you struggle with feedback, your relationships are strained, you blame others for your failures, you never feel satisfied, you ask too much and give too little, and/or you don't hire people smarter than you. It's all about you and your problems, your stress, and your burdens. You might not even know you're doing these things because your ego keeps you in the dark and discourages you from the type of exploration that could lead to more self-awareness. At an organizational level, companies run by leaders with overactive egos struggle with innovation and growth because everyone is afraid to approach, much less confront, their boss's ego. They know they're only going to have their head bitten off—so why say anything? Remember that leadership disconnect I mentioned earlier? An ego in overdrive is a big contributor to this problem. Even self-aware people find themselves in the dark about internal chokeholds on their thoughts or behaviors. With every new step forward, a new gap opens up. If you're moving towards new possibilities, there's always a gap between what got you here to what is needed to get there.

So, now that we're clear who's really in charge (your ego), let's figure out how to change things. Remember, the ego likes to react in the moment, not plan for the future. You'll need to be very intentional about managing your ego. Richard Rohr, founder of the Center for Action and Contemplation, put it this way: "The human ego prefers anything, just about anything, to failing, or changing, or dying. The ego is that part of you that loves the status quo—even when it's not working. It attaches to the past and present and fears the future."

If you allow an overactive ego to guide your decision making at work, it's going to be very challenging to lead people into a successful future—indeed, it's going to be very challenging to lead them at all!

You're choosing to stay on the train even though the bridge ahead is out. This won't end well for you or your people. Your ego will keep you mired in problems and stuck in a place of hopelessness, fear, and frustration. Your human system will be frozen, unable to productively figure out what to do, while the train keeps barreling toward the cliff ahead. The world doesn't stop just because you and your team aren't capable of addressing the problems ahead. Becoming agile enough to respond together in the moment means leaving your overactive ego on the shelf.

If you have any of the symptoms of an overactive ego—and we all do—stop now and do the work. It's time for you to be in charge, not your ego. Don't be a roadblock to your own effective leadership. Are you ready to leave your saboteur (lowest-ego self) at home and bring your higher self to work? Great! Please step into my office (or someone else's) and let down your defenses. I believe that you're brave enough to break the stranglehold your ego has on your potential. It will take courage and resolve, but you won't be alone. We're on the same side. Now let's get to work.

Change Takes Courage

From here on out, you will be thinking and acting differently. You'll be proactive instead of reactive—even when things look dire. Courage means trusting your abilities to do whatever it takes, even if that means trying things that might not work and learning from those failures. When your ego is no longer in charge and you've committed to a growth mindset, everything becomes possible. As Johan Wolfgang von Goethe once famously said, "At the moment of commitment, the entire universe conspires to assist you." It's true. I've seen it happen for those who have the courage to believe it.

Now that you're not being led around by your wounded ego, you can start authentically engaging and openly contributing. People will react to your new openness by being more open with you. You'll focus more on your people and your organization's strengths, not its limitations. This will evolve into genuine exploration of innovative ideas—and they'll no longer have to be *your* ideas. You'll find you're yelling less and listening more. You'll stop blaming others and instead start problem solving with them. You'll welcome a diversity of perspectives and find deeper meaning in orchestrating an environment where the varied voices and energies of your people can blend into a seamless synergistic whole. It won't happen overnight, but these are the characteristics of a high-performance leader *and* culture. This is an environment of endless potential and creativity where people can feel significant and do meaningful work. This is not a combative space where egos rule but a collaborative one where self-actualization isn't only possible but highly probable.

Why Do You Get Up in the Morning?

For many people, the answer to this question is "I have to get the kids off to school" or "I have to go to work." They live in a world of doing, not being. If your knee-jerk answer is similar, it's time for some self-reflection about your "why." Moving from responsibility to responsibility without a guiding vision is like living on a hamster wheel. It's not going to take you anywhere new or exciting—same old, same old. It might *feel* like you're in motion, but you're actually in a rut. And, if *you* are on a hamster wheel, your company probably is as well. Explore your *personal* values—not your company's values—*your* values, what *you* believe. This is foundational work that can change your personal and professional life. In fact, it's the foundation for *everything*.

When people talk about CEOs truly dedicated to operating companies in alignment with their personal values, Patagonia and its visionary founder Yvon Chouinard often lead the conversation. Chouinard is the son of a French Canadian handyman and grew up as an avid climber, surfer, and environmentalist. He started

Patagonia simply to create better equipment and clothing for the life he led. Baked into that lifestyle was a profound respect for nature. This was his noble cause and became the ethos of his company. As Chouinard matured as the company's first CEO, his belief system drove innovation, attracted the right people and customers (those aligned with his values), and resulted in tremendous growth. If you want to study what it looks like to have a noble cause and well-defined core values embedded into the DNA of a company, read a couple of Chouinard's books. I recommend *Let My People Go Surfing* and *The Responsible Company*.

Chouinard's eco-conscious outdoor clothing company is committed to using business to protect nature. This is not always easy to do when you're a sixty-year-old global company generating more than $1 billion in annual revenue. But, somehow, they pull it off year after year—not with lip service but with intentional action— and their loyal customers keep coming back for more. In 2021, the company's Black Friday event reached a record-breaking $10 million in sales—five times higher than predicted for that single-day event. Patagonia donated *all of it* to hundreds of local environmental organizations around the world. Their customers called it a "fundraiser for the earth."

Patagonia's success story demonstrates that, when a company operates with a noble cause and in harmony with an authentic set of corporate values, optimal performance and growth are achievable. This means *all* the humans in the organization are committed to these values. Do you think people who simply get out bed to go to work can do the kind of amazing and purposeful work that Patagonia's human system is achieving? Patagonia wouldn't be the company it is today without a leader who understood exactly why he got out of bed each morning. During his tenure as CEO at Patagonia, Chouinard embodied his mission and values at work each day. He attracted like-minded people to help him build a company aligned with his values—and theirs. These people could collaborate and problem solve together because they understood the importance of their work and how it clearly supported their personal and professional values. They were all committed to a shared mission, a common purpose, a noble cause. Even on the bad days, their company's leaders lived by the values they all treasured.

The majority of US companies, and their leaders, aren't operating in alignment with a noble cause or strong set of values. In fact, a 2021 LRN ethics study found the opposite: one in four interviewed employees said that, in the past six months, they had witnessed unethical, and even illegal, behavior where they work. Chances are most of the leaders at the companies in question had paid plenty of lip service to values but weren't walking the talk. Unfortunately, a *lack* of values is the more common scenario in corporate America. Research by the *MIT Sloan Management Review* indicates that 80 percent of the seven hundred large companies they studied had published an official set of corporate values on their website. They discussed their findings in the 2020 article "When It Comes to Culture, Does Your Company Walk the Talk?"

> Over the past three decades, more than three-quarters of CEOs interviewed in a major business magazine discussed their company's culture or core values—even when not specifically asked about it.

> Corporate values statements are nearly universal, but do they matter? Critics dismiss them as cheap talk with no impact on employees' day-to-day behavior. Recent corporate scandals support the skeptics' view. Volkswagen, Wells Fargo, and Barclays each included ethics or integrity among their core values in the years before their wrongdoings were discovered, while Boeing hit the trifecta by listing integrity, quality, and safety among its "enduring values."

We've already explored the cultural meltdown at Volkswagen, but one need only search a couple of business news sites to see the headlines associated with bad corporate behavior at Wells Fargo, Barclays, and Boeing. So, how do companies like Patagonia rise above? How do they actually create a culture that lives and breathes ethical behavior guided by a core set of values—and do so sustainably and profitably? It can't be easy, right? You might be asking, "Who leads such transformation? Would my company's people widely adopt a core-values initiative? How would we measure success? How long and how much money would it take?" These are all valid C-suite questions. But, if this is what is swirling around in your head, you're looking at this challenge from the wrong angle: the outside in. Flip your perspective and start looking at problems from the inside out.

A Human Guiding a Human System

A noble cause and a specific and unique set of core values guide *everything* and *everyone* at Patagonia. When team members discovered the cotton used to make Patagonia's clothing was grown and harvested with harmful chemicals and unsustainable practices, they quickly shifted to organic cotton. Anyone in manufacturing would cringe at the complexity of this type of change. At the time, such a shift was unprecedented, but that didn't stop Chouinard's team. Once they realized regular cotton clashed with their core values, the decision was clear and swift. Everyone at every level in the company supported the move, despite the challenges. CEO Yvon Chouinard was not only on board; he led the charge. And *that* is exactly how Patagonia rises above and creates a high-performance culture. The individuals in this human system live and breathe a shared vision of and commitment to their company's noble purpose and the values that support it.

Perhaps you're thinking, *While Chouinard's idealism is all well and good, he was a founder. He was able to shape Patagonia's values and culture from the beginning. I'm not a founder. I've also got to deal with my board, our investors, a global pandemic, and an ever-shifting economy. I'm an ethical person, and I believe in certain values, but I don't have a life's passion like Chouinard.* Keep thinking that way and you're not likely to get very far. That's your ego talking again—and holding you back. Satya Nadella is a great example of someone who has successfully orchestrated transformative change around a new set of values at Microsoft, even though he was the company's third CEO.

The work you're undertaking is of great importance, but, as I've mentioned, it's not easy. You're going to discover things that will surprise and even upset you, so be kind to yourself on the journey. So, how does the journey begin? With a crucial conversation with the leader within. *You must understand yourself before you can successfully lead others.* Becoming more self-aware and being crystal clear about your calling in life and personal values is the right place to start, the only place to start.

Many of the world's top leadership experts—Ken Blanchard, Patrick Lencioni, and Stephen Covey, to name a few—teach that deeper self-awareness is more crucial for success than ever. Why does this extraordinary brain trust believe this? Because, as mentioned earlier, companies are human systems. You can't successfully "deal with" any of your stressors without having your people on board to help. Everyone must navigate the stormy seas together if your company is going to safely arrive at its desired destination. Like a rudder steers a boat, you're the person who shows everyone where the company is headed and how you're all going to safely navigate there. But how can you steer the boat for others if you're not captain of your own ship? Think about basic safety training. The trainers always tell you to help yourself before helping others. You've certainly been on an airplane and been told in emergencies to put the oxygen mask on yourself before placing it on the child in the seat next you.

Lifeguards learn to put the life vest on themselves before going out into deep water to save others. If you don't prepare in this specific order—saving yourself first—there's a good chance both parties will lose. That's why understanding yourself, your ultimate purpose and values, should be your highest priority as a leader. The time to start this important work is now. There can be no higher priority.

You know well that the only constant in business is that things constantly change. Surprises and challenges are always just around the next corner. Be prepared. Strengthen yourself so you can strengthen your leadership team and organizational culture. Whether your company is struggling—with growth, problem solving, ethical behavior, innovation, people, etc.—or trying to break through to the next level, I promise the solution starts with you. No matter how expert you are in your industry, how high your IQ, or how many years of experience you have, you can't have sustained success unless you can effectively lead yourself and others on a journey of continuous improvement, self-awareness, and personal growth in alignment with a strong mission and clear core values. Take the necessary time. Strengthen the leader within. Become the master of your own universe so you can lead others to bring about the change that is needed in your organization.

This journey of self-discovery begins with you finding and committing to your ultimate purpose, your reason for being, and then identifying *your* values—those that empower you to behave in service to that purpose and be the person that you want to be day in and day out in the face of anything. But as bestselling author Nir Eyal wrote on his blog nirandfar.com, values are much more than what you care about:

> What we care about changes every day—every minute, even—and that's why it's hard to agree on common values. When your kid is throwing a tantrum, you care about getting some peace and quiet. When you're stuck in bumper-to-bumper traffic

with an empty fuel tank, you care about whether there's a gas station nearby. But these things are not your values.

Why? Because values are more forward-thinking than simply reactions to the immediate moment. They are attributes of the person you want to be.

For example, kindness is one of my values. Every day, I will try to embody that attribute. And if I'm kind to people, then I know I'm living according to my value of kindness. Money, on the other hand, is not one of my values. Rather, money is a thing I value, and there are many ways to get it. One way is doing a job and getting paid for it. Another way is mugging a guy who's wearing an expensive watch. Only one of those methods is compatible with my value of kindness.

Here's a simple test: If someone can take it away from you, then it's not one of your values.

Can you articulate your highest purpose and personal values? Do you understand how your values were shaped? How do you hold yourself accountable to live in alignment with your values? How have your values shaped you? Where could your values take you in life? These are the types of questions to ask yourself. Your answers provide a foundation to create an inspiring and transformative personal vision and, later, a leadership vision for your company. Who is the person you want to become? What does it feel like when you're living according to your values? As Stephen Covey wrote in his bestselling book *The 7 Habits of Highly Effective People*, "Begin with the end in mind." Start being your highest self and bringing that person to work every day. Everything else will follow.

Far too many people, allow themselves to be defined by their work. When things are going right, life feels good and happy. When things go wrong, many people fall apart. If everything you are is tied up in your company and position, then you're in deep trouble. When you don't have a bigger purpose driven by your personal values, you will always fall victim to outside circumstance. Like an unmoored boat, you'll be tossed around by each wave, unable to move forward in your personal or professional life. Commit to operating according to your values, purpose, and personal vision. Everyone gets off track sometimes. The key is to learn how to recognize that you are off track and quickly recalibrate.

If you haven't done this type of work before, you'll soon realize that it takes intention to begin living in such a self-reflective state. After you understand your purpose and values, you get to commit to living in alignment with those values each day. This means being much more mindful about what you think, say, and do in everyday situations. If you wake up in the morning and say you value kindness like Nir Eyal, that's a great start. But, if you go to the office, get a bad quarterly financial report, and start reprimanding people, you're not being kind or honoring kindness as one of your core values. You're out of alignment, and that will come back to bite you. This is why it's important to *plan* to think and act differently. This will increase your chances of living in alignment with your values, especially when the going gets tough. In business, you're much more likely to execute successfully when you have a *plan*. The same thing is required to live by your core values. If kindness is one of your values, you must wake up each morning and *think* about why it's important to be kind and then *plan* out how you'll be kind throughout the day. You must *believe* that you're capable of kindness and *act* on this belief. You must *practice* kindness in all that you do, especially under stressful circumstances. You must model kindness toward those around you.

Think. Plan. Believe. Act. Practice. Repeat.

When you choose to live in alignment with your values and commit to learning how to do so, your thoughts and behaviors improve, your life is enriched, and you are better prepared to lead your company into a brighter future.

Living in Alignment

I'm a big believer in writing down what's important. There's a permanence to it. That's why, when you're ready, I encourage you to write a personal vision statement to document your values, clarify who you are as your best self, and define what successful living and leadership look like to you. This statement will guide your choices and ensure you spend time and energy on the right things and with the right people. Afterall, the way you spend your time is a reflection of what matters most to you, and the people you spend it with shape who you are. You'll start to operate at your full potential and achieve your most important goals, both as an individual and a leader.

Now that you've written your personal vision statement and committed to living in alignment with your mission, vision, and values, you're able to call upon the true leader within. Think about what it might look like if you brought this better version of yourself to the office every day. What could happen if you operated at your highest level throughout the work week? You're likely to be more proactive than reactive. You're likely to command more respect and trust because you're thinking, acting, and living according to your values. You're likely to be less ego driven and more focused on the needs of others. You're likely to be more approachable because your behavior will be more predictable and your demeanor calmer. These changes alone are likely to sow the seeds of transformation.

But let's take this a step further. Hopefully, once you've written your personal vision statement, you're ready to write a professional leadership intention statement to bring your personal mission, vision, and values into your work life. When you closely align your personal and professional lives, your days feel much more balanced, productive, and rewarding.

I've done this work myself. As I've grown as a person and a leader, I've come to understand that my calling is to liberate the human spirit. This is what I discovered when I brought my personal values into my business and aligned them with my leadership vision. This is what gets me out of bed in the morning and shapes everything I do. It's what inspires me and gives my work and life meaning. This foundation has shaped my company's values and helped us innovate and grow substantially. As a result of this work, I'm no longer continually taken on a roller coaster ride of emotions when it comes to the ups and downs of business. Now, for the most part, I am anchored, confident, and committed to my mission. I can see the lighthouse, even in stormy weather, and so can my people. Why? Because I'm in continuous personal development and modeling our values every day.

This is how it works. This is why all transformation begins with you. Do the personal work. Discover your values and live by them. Align those values with your leadership at work. Walk the talk. Model what you believe in. Your people will notice. It will change how they see you and the company you lead. Then, together, you can take all this to your partners and customers. Now, as a human system, your company is ready to serve them at the highest level.

None of us is perfect. Life can be unpredictable and being human outright messy. Even with the best intentions, we veer off course—I know I do. But, when you get used to compassionate self-assessment, you quickly recognize the misalignments, apologize if needed, and recalibrate. The ability to course correct is what is most important. You no longer get stuck, nor do the people around you. That's why discovering your highest purpose and core values as a person, leader, and company is not a one-time exercise. It's a lifelong commitment—a new way of being. Healthy, successful adults lead and live from the inside out. They understand themselves and their values and commit to ongoing growth and improvement. Their work doesn't define them. Rather, their values define their work. And *this* makes all the difference.

KEY TAKEAWAYS

- Fear equals resistance, which is the enemy of change.
- Explore, articulate, and align your life with your highest purpose and personal values. This is important, foundational work and a life-long commitment.
- You must do the personal work before you can help others.

BRAINHACK

The best way to get out of a fight-or-flight response is by taking long, conscious breaths. Exhaling stimulates the vagus nerve, which is one of the main nerves in the parasympathetic nervous system. The parasympathetic nervous system controls the "rest and digest" functions in our bodies and can pull us out of any type of anger or fear response. Exhaling in particular is what activates your vagus nerve and calms you down. Try taking five deep breaths, breathing in for four, holding for two, and exhaling for six. Another quick way to stimulate the vagus nerve is by plugging your right nostril and taking breaths in and out through your left. The parasympathetic nervous system corresponds to your left nostril and your sympathetic to your right. If you want more energy, do the same thing but only breathe through your right nostril.

POWERFUL QUESTIONS

- What is resonating for you in this chapter?
- What are your defined values?
- What would be possible if your values and highest purpose were aligned?

CHAPTER 4

Your People Need
YOU in the Room!

*"Always hold fast to the present. Every situation,
indeed every moment, is of infinite value, for it
is the representative of a whole eternity."*

—— JOHANN WOLFGANG VON GOETHE ——

D espite a late-night business meeting the evening before, Donna was already waiting for her Uber curbside by 7:00 a.m. She might not have had a great night's sleep due to the three-hour time difference, but she'd still made it to her 5:00 a.m. workout at the hotel gym. The protein power bar in her bag and large cup of black coffee would give her the immediate boost of clarity and energy she needed. There was still much to do before the 8:00 a.m. with her management team. She was no stranger to this juggling act, so she knew she'd be fine. She hopped in the Uber, nodded at the driver with a short, warm smile, then got down to work. Coffee in left hand, tablet on her lap, and cell phone in her right hand, she plowed through emails, personal and professional texts, the morning's headlines on CNN, and a couple of LinkedIn posts and then

41

responded to a number of important Slack messages. A few minutes before pulling into the conference center, she took her final sip of coffee, quickly reviewed the meeting agenda, and made a couple of final notes. As the CEO of a thriving ecommerce company, she knew she was at her best when multitasking on tight deadlines. Adrenaline was her best friend.

"Good morning, everyone." She smiled as she strode confidently into the room at 7:59. "How's everyone enjoying winter in New York?" There was a vaguely positive murmur from the group. "I agree. Brrrr! But the tradeshow is going quite well. Strong sales. Just give me a moment to wrap up these last few messages and I'll be right with you." Donna sat at the head of the conference table and pulled out her laptop as she read something on her phone. The rest of the team worked quietly. The room was filled with busy, productive professionals typing or reading on cell phones, tablets, and laptops.

"Thanks for your patience, everyone. Shall we begin? John, you're up first." A few people looked up, but most kept working. John spoke for a few minutes uninterrupted, except for two questions from Donna, who asked them while looking at her computer.

"Thanks, John. Anyone have any final questions?" Donna saw a few heads shake as she scanned the room. "Great. Janice, you're up next. Business development update, right?"

"Actually, I transitioned over to marketing a few weeks ago, Donna, so I'll be talking about our latest influencer campaign."

"That's right. Of course. We're all looking forward to your report, Janice." All eyes downward, the room full of heads bobbed in agreement amid a quiet hum of activity. Smart and skilled, Janice presented an impeccable PowerPoint packed with insights and relevant graphics. No one was making eye contact with her, so she hoped someone was noticing her hard work.

"We do have an issue, Donna," Janice said. "One of our top brand ambassadors has moved over to Brandnext. I reached out to her yesterday, and she told me that Brandnext's new features fit her needs better, and they are paying influencers way more than we are."

"Brandnext?" Donna looked up, confused. "That little startup out of Atlanta?"

"Yes," Janice replied. "They secured a $60-million-round a few months ago, and they're growing rapidly."

Everyone looked up at once, but no one said a word.

"How come I didn't know anything about this?" Donna snapped. She scanned the room as heads quickly tipped back downward toward device screens. "Janice?"

"I believe Brandon brought this up in our last meeting, Donna, but something came up, and you had to leave. He's been trying to get on your calendar ever since."

"Brandon." Donna was standing now. "Let's get that meeting scheduled today, okay?"

"Absolutely!" Brandon snapped to attention.

"Okay, people, we've got work to do." Now irritated and stressed, Donna was already packing up her laptop to head out to the trade-show floor. "We'll reconvene tomorrow to finish the rest of the reports. We've got a fire to put out."

Within the next year, Donna's company would lose 10 percent market share and struggle to innovate on their once-bestselling product.

The Adrenaline Bias

I know many leaders like Donna—too many, in fact. In today's world, everyone is busy—all of the time. Technology has enabled us to connect and communicate with one another quickly and frequently through dozens of platforms and devices. It has also enabled us to accomplish more in less time, increasing our productivity—at least that's how it feels. So we keep cramming more tasks into the same number of hours in the day, keeping our brains constantly on the move.

But here's the truth: multitasking is a myth. Just look at distracted driver laws enacted to alter the dangerous behavior of those who think they can safely text and drive. They cannot. Distracted driving causes more than three thousand deaths per year and two hundred eighty thousand injuries. That's a pretty clear-cut indictment of multitasking. Yet, somehow, we behave as if our brains will work differently in a conference room. They don't.

If you've ever been in a meeting like the one above—and I'm guessing that you have—you've witnessed what leadership guru Patrick Lencioni calls "the adrenaline bias." People are so hooked on working at a feverish pace, they have trouble stopping, reflecting, and truly listening to one another. Today, more and more people struggle with addiction to this adrenaline high, making it challenging to be fully engaged in, or even fully present for, the activities, conversations, and experiences right in front of them. Our bodies might be physically in the room, but our minds are flitting all over the place. It's a big problem.

Over the past couple of decades, the adrenaline bias—or what behavioral and organizational psychologists call cognitive scattering or scattered-brain syndrome—has had a profound impact on human behavior, thinking, and interactions. And, since companies are human systems, this is an important shift that every business leader needs to understand. One study, highlighted in a BBC article about scattered-brain syndrome, found that "knowledge workers are interrupted every three minutes by email and other distractions, lowering their overall ability to get anything done. The study estimates that such disruptions cost a company of fifty thousand employees about $1 billion in lost time, reduced creativity, errors, and burnout."

Companies tend to blame the individual employee for burnout, but the issue is much deeper than this, as Eric Garton, author of *Time, Talent and Energy*, points out in his *Harvard Business Review* article entitled, "Employee Burnout Is a Problem with the Company, Not the Person":

> When employees aren't as productive as they could be, it's usually the organization, not its employees, that is to blame. The same is true for employee burnout. When we looked inside companies with high burnout rates, we saw three common culprits: excessive collaboration, weak time management disciplines, and a tendency to overload the most capable with too much work. These forces not only rob employees of time to concentrate on completing complex tasks or for idea generation, they also crunch the downtime that is necessary for restoration.

Let me take Garton's point a step further and say that employee distraction is a cultural issue and, as such, a leadership issue. If you're a company executive battling your own adrenaline addiction, how are you going to help your people battle theirs? You can't. Our multitasking CEO Donna provides a perfect example of how a leader sets the tone for a company's behavior. To change your culture and the behavior of your people, you have to get your own house in order first. Let's dive into some basic neuroscience to begin.

- **The prefrontal cortex** stores our learned competencies and guides complex cognitive behaviors, personality expression, values, and executive function. It also moderates our social behaviors.

- **The cerebral cortex** is associated with higher-level processes, such as consciousness, reasoning, language, and memory.
- **The amygdala** processes threatening stimuli, activates the fight-or-flight mechanism, and attaches emotional significance to events or memories.

Think of the prefrontal and cerebral cortex as areas for higher-level, proactive, conscious thinking and behaviors, while the amygdala is primarily a place for more basic, reactive, unconscious thoughts and behaviors. We need both but for different circumstances—and that's where things have become tricky in our busy modern world.

Above- and Below-the-Line Traits

When you're the busy leader of a growing company, it can be easy to miss the impact of small, daily thoughts and behaviors exhibited and communicated by you, your leadership team, and your people. But make no mistakes, this is exactly what is shaping your culture for better or worse—not the quarterly meetings, white papers, or latest initiative. With this in mind, let's take a look at some above-the-line and below-the-line traits in order to zero in on positive and negative behaviors. Positive, above-the-line-behaviors include respect, hope, curiosity, connection, cooperation, openness, compassion, joy, tolerance, courage, trust, and many others. Negative, below-the-line traits include scarcity, shame, righteousness, doubt, dominance, anger, cynicism, manipulation, jealousy, hatred, an us-versus-them mentality, and so forth. Become aware of your above-the-line and below-the-line behaviors and those of your colleagues. This is where your culture lives in these daily behaviors. If you're seeing a lot of below-the-line behaviors, it might be time for some personal self-reflection and development as well as an organization-wide cultural reset.

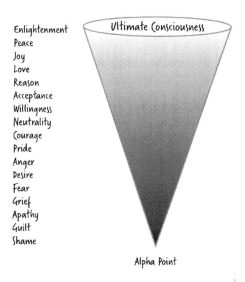

Enlightenment
Peace
Joy
Love
Reason
Acceptance
Willingness
Neutrality
Courage
Pride
Anger
Desire
Fear
Grief
Apathy
Guilt
Shame

Ultimate Consciousness

Alpha Point

The human brain is truly amazing. It can process more than eleven million bits of information per second (bps). However, our conscious mind can only handle 40 to 50 bps. And, while we're trying to process all those bits of information, we're also having thoughts—up to sixty thousand thoughts per day, with 85 percent of them negative or repetitive. It's like a war going on in our brains! To manage everything, our brain takes shortcuts that allow us to make decisions quickly rather than get bogged down and overwhelmed by all those data inputs. Adrenaline and cortisol facilitate these shortcuts. Primarily secreted by the adrenal glands, these stress hormones prepare our bodies physically and mentally to take action. In the early days of our evolution, we needed this shortcut frequently to avoid being eaten by a predator. Acting fast was a matter of survival. Today, this early brain wiring is still useful in certain situations. Adrenaline and cortisol can get us pumped up to run a race, for example, or win a game, avoid or flee a dangerous situation, or meet our sales goals. But these stress hormones can also hijack our brains, instigate breakdowns in communications, and wreak havoc on how we listen and interpret situations. All too often, this results in strained relationships and poor decision-making.

The amygdala is the part of the brain that manages these short-cuts and sets in motion a series of events that trigger the production of adrenaline and cortisol. When the amygdala senses fear or an imminent threat, it instantly goes into the fight-or-flight response before the conscious, reasoning part of the brain, the cerebral cortex, can overrule it. As the center of our emotional processing, the amygdala kicks into high gear when we need spontaneous, unconscious reactions—what we call our gut instincts. It quickly matches the current situation to preexisting stereotypes and templates shaped by our experiences, family, friends, community, culture, religion, the media, and so on. Most of the time, we don't even realize these influences are in play. Unfortunately, in today's rushed, multitasking world, our brain often gets confused. It senses anxiety from the daily juggling act and engages the amygdala when it's not needed. Adrenaline and cortisol hormones rush in, and the templates come into play—in the form of habituated patterns—even when there's no real threat. We keep rushing and trying to navigate stressful meetings and tight deadlines. Instead of helping us, these powerful evolutionary mechanisms end up distracting us, clouding our judgment, and causing us to take inappropriate actions.

These misfires have become a very real issue. More than thirty-seven million Americans take some type of antidepressant or anxiety medication to balance their brain chemistry—and that number keeps growing. As our brains keep racing around and are pulled in multiple directions, deep work, focus, authentic human connection, and meaningful strategic thinking are all being compromised. Amygdala hijacking and cognitive scattering are a growing concern for today's companies, especially if it's a caffeine-fueled, adrenaline-seeking culture like the one Donna has created.

If Donna's style of leadership sounds anything like yours, it's time to ask yourself an important question: is the adrenaline high going to take you and your company where you want to go? I can tell you from twenty-five years of experience that the answer is no. Your company is not in a sprint; it's in a marathon. You're not being chased by a predator; you're building an intentional roadmap for high performance and growth. Adrenaline might have gotten you and your team successfully out of the gate or even launched you into high-growth mode, but, over time, it will hinder the type of strategic, proactive thinking necessary to create and sustain a culture where breakthrough performance is the norm, not the exception. For this, you need the more proactive parts of your brain in control. If you're a victim of amygdala hijack, you must retrain your brain so that it stops functioning in a constant state of crisis and becomes fully present.

Your Presence Is Requested

Much has been written about the importance of executive presence—a leader's ability to inspire confidence and command the room. It's a crucial skill, but it's not what I'm talking about here. Executive presence is an outside-in construct. For example, if you need to become a better public speaker to improve your executive presence, you can sign up for Toastmasters. It's a great group, and they can help you learn and master this important executive skill—very straightforward. What I'm talking about in this chapter is an inside-out effort—the idea of relearning how to *be* in the world and fully engage in all of life's unique moments, both big and small. This is an exercise in mindfulness and awareness. Let's break it down into four key areas for development:

1. **Focus on full presence.** As we witnessed in Donna's story, many people live in a state of constant distraction. In fact, a major study at Harvard that looked at 2,250 subjects and a quarter-million data points concluded that people weren't fully engaged in the task in front of them a whopping 47 percent of the time. More interestingly, mind-wandering was found to be an excellent predictor of people's happiness.

49

The more present a subject was—engaged in the task at hand—the happier they described themselves to researchers. The less present they were, the more unhappy. The modern world has made it more challenging to live fully in the present moment, and this has negatively impacted our well-being. In fact, another twenty-year Harvard study of six thousand men and women aged twenty-five to seventy-four found that "emotional vitality—a sense of enthusiasm, of hopefulness, of engagement in life, and the ability to face life's stresses with emotional balance—appears to reduce the risk of coronary heart disease." It's part of a growing body of research showing a strong link between our thoughts and emotions and our physical and mental well-being. Forward-looking companies like Google have taken note of this correlation and adapted their organizational cultures to encourage creativity and well-being. In 2007, an engineer at Google named Chade-Meng Tan gathered a team of leading experts in mindfulness techniques, neuroscience, leadership, and emotional intelligence to develop an internal course called "Search Inside Yourself" (SIY). It was designed to help fellow Googlers "develop the skills of mindfulness, empathy, and overall emotional intelligence to create the conditions for individual and collective thriving." The program was so successful that it has become the Search Inside Yourself Leadership Institute. Though now independent, the team still works with Google, as well as many other high-performance organizations, such as SAP, the United Nations, Procter & Gamble, and Salesforce, among others.

2. **Embrace childlike wonder.** As very young children, we are completely immersed in the world around us. We are constantly observing, interacting, and learning. Our senses are fully engaged. We have endless curiosity. We might become fascinated with a worm or a butterfly or a dandelion.

We ask a lot of questions. Why does the sun come up in the morning? How do people get taller? What's bigger than an elephant? Why does my brother have blue eyes when mine are brown? We question everything because we exist in a constant state of exploration. We try . . . we stumble . . . we learn . . . we grow . . . we try again . . . we stumble . . . we learn . . . we keep growing. No judgement. No regret. That's just the day-to-day life of the average toddler. Youngsters are never bored because the world is full of wonder and opportunities to explore. But, somewhere along the way, this changes. As we age, we become less observant, more disengaged, and more set in our ways. We get so used to our daily routines and surroundings that we stop noticing them. Our sense of childlike wonder goes into hibernation. We may be more mature, but we're less fully alive. Through intentional work, this slide into going through the motions can be reversed, and that childlike spirit of wonder can be reawakened. There's nothing childish about childlike wonder. It's an energy source worth your attention as a leader.

3. **Master sensory acuity.** This concept came out of a psychological approach developed in the 1970s at the University of California, Santa Cruz, called neuro-linguistic programming (NLP). It involves analyzing and applying strategies used by successful individuals to reach personal goals. NLP relates to thoughts, language, and patterns of behavior and seeks to build effective communication between conscious and unconscious mental processes to help people increase their creativity and problem-solving skills. As part of NLP, sensory acuity is about learning to use all our senses to observe the world closely and carefully in order to gather detailed information about the present moment. Sensory acuity is also important for human interactions because people's body language is always sharing important clues

about our emotions and thoughts. In fact, words make up only 7 percent of human communication, while tonality makes up 38 percent, and physiology (think body language) accounts for 55 percent. Those who master sensory acuity learn to observe other people's physiology, which is a precursor to empathy. Imagine you're talking to someone on your executive team about a challenge. How might your reaction and behavior change if you could fully tune in to that person's smallest changes in skin color, muscle tone, eye contact, and breathing? Sensory acuity is about reading the person in front of you and reading the room around you. It's a powerful skill that can only be learned by those who know how to be fully present in the moment.

4. **Develop rapport.** Defined simply as a close, harmonious relationship between two or more people, rapport is critical in both our personal and professional lives. It's about creating deep, authentic relationships where people work to understand and respect the feelings and values of others. As world-renown motivational speaker Tony Robbins describes it, "building rapport helps to achieve mutual trust and understanding. . . . It leads to deep listening, meaningful conversations, and fulfilling relationships where everyone involved benefits. . . . When it comes to understanding how to build rapport for communication purposes, your first step is taking inventory of your personality. By getting in touch with your communication and leadership style, you're able to connect with your truest self, which is the cornerstone of building rapport." Like everything else we've covered in this book, the work always begins with ourselves before it expands to others.

Mastering these four behavioral shifts takes time, practice, focused energy, patience, commitment, and compassion. Overcoming our brain's evolutionary wiring and years of ingrained patterns of thinking and behaving can be pretty intense work. But the results will enrich your life and leadership in ways you've never imagined.

Meaningful Listening

Once you begin to master these four skills, you'll understand what it feels like to live and work naturally in a state of full presence. You'll experience its profound benefits and want to practice presence in everything you do. One of the biggest changes you'll see is the way you listen. There are many reasons *why* we listen. Perhaps we're trying to gather information, learn something new, or develop rapport. But it's *how* we listen that's more important. In his bestselling book *The 7 Habits of Highly Effective People*, author Stephen Covey outlines the five levels of listening:

1. **Ignoring**—when there is no effort from the listener due to distractions or a lack of caring about what the speaker has to say.
2. **Pretend Listening**—when the listener is fairly disengaged and says things like, "Uh-huh," "That's good," or "Really?" The listener isn't absorbing the information the speaker is sharing.
3. **Selective**—when the listener filters out information that doesn't interest them or doesn't conform to their biases and preconceived notions.
4. **Attentive Listening**—when the listener is engaged and evaluates the information being spoken in order to determine whether they agree or disagree. The listener is also assessing how the information applies to them.
5. **Active or Empathetic Listening**—when the listener is fully present and focused on the speaker's words and what those words mean not only to them but to the speaker. The listener

is giving their whole being to the conversation. This is the highest and most meaningful level of listening.

As you master the art of being fully present, you might notice that you're becoming a more active, more empathetic listener. You're fully tuned into your people. You hear and remember what they say. You begin to sense what's behind their words and what's driving them to speak and behave in certain ways. This will allow you to operate from a higher level as a leader—more intuitively. Over time, and with consistent and ongoing practice, this fundamental shift toward complete presence begins to transform your life, your leadership, and your business. Be present for yourself. Be present for your people. You need them and they need you—all of you—in the room.

KEY TAKEAWAYS

- Watch out for the adrenaline bias and how it might be hijacking your brain and your company's culture.
- Practice being completely present in everything you do. Do your best to eliminate as many distractions as possible. Demonstrate what this looks like for your people.
- Explore why you do or don't listen to someone. Shed your biases, learn how to listen meaningfully, and learn active, empathetic listening.

BRAINHACK

Our brains have a limit to how much stress we can take. Here is an easy way to visualize this. Say you have a bucket in your brain, and, every time something stressful happens, it goes into that bucket. Not getting enough sleep? Bucket. Not eating right? Bucket. Stressed at work? Bucket. Constantly on an adrenaline high? Bucket. All the little stressors in your life add to the bucket until one day the bucket is full. When this happens, your brain will induce a threat response. This response can come in the form of physical or emotional pain, illness, burnout, or anything that will make you stop. If you ignore the signal, it keeps getting worse. Often, when people experience chronic pain at work, it is because their bucket is constantly too full. People who enjoy their jobs tend to experience less work-related pain. But there are easy ways to empty your bucket—breathing meditation, a proper nights sleep, moving your body, eating something healthy, taking a break from work, and allowing your brain to recover. The less threat you have in the bucket, the easier you will be able to handle life. All these things will empty your bucket and increase your ability to cope with the stress of the world. Your brain wants to protect you—listen to it.

POWERFUL QUESTIONS

- What is resonating for you in this chapter?
- Where is your adrenaline bias showing up at work?
- What's the impact on you and others?
- What would it mean for you to deepen how you listen?

CHAPTER 5

Are You Ready to Model a Growth Mindset?

"Live as if you were to die to tomorrow;
learn as if you were to live forever."

— MAHATMA GANDHI —

ax was flabbergasted. *How could she?* he thought. His legal startup was booming. He could barely keep up with the demand, but he'd just lost another account executive. Sarah was the third top producer to leave in a year. But this departure hurt more than the others. He knew Sarah was the best hire he had ever made—and he had hired a lot of people in his hard-driving thirty-five years in business. He wasn't some novice startup CEO. He had built numerous profitable companies and built them fast. He was in the process of doing it again, but this time the turnover was killing him. He'd even made Sarah a partner to show her how much he believed in her ability to drive his company forward. The more revenue she could produce, the more generously she would be rewarded. *Why would she walk away from such a great deal?* he wondered.

"Damn millennials," he grumbled. "Too much coddling. Too much attention. I'm over it."

Max shared the whole sorry story with me on our weekly call.

"Where did she take a job?" I asked.

"Some firm out in the suburbs. Said she wanted a strong community and more work-life balance. I think she even took a pay cut! I don't get it, Magi. What do these young people want?"

"Different things than you, it seems, Max. What's your next step?"

"Well, I'm not hiring any more millennials or Gen X, Y, or Z-ers, I can tell you that!"

I laughed and shook my head. "Max, as the saying goes, the only constant in life is change. We *all* have to keep learning and adapting. Young professionals are taking a different approach to . . ."

"Magi, I'm tired of learning," he interrupted. "I'm good at what I do. I'm *very* successful. I don't want to change. *They* can change if they want to work for me. I just need to find the right people."

Max is a great guy. But, in that moment, I knew he was in trouble unless he changed his mindset. When everyone else is wrong and you're the only "right" person in the room, there's a problem. In Max's view, he was right, and Sarah was wrong. Where did this thinking get him? Nowhere. She had left along with the others.

I knew Max would keep bleeding people if he didn't adapt. He wasn't listening to what his top talent was telling him. He wasn't hearing what they wanted or needed. It was his way or the highway—so, one by one, they all chose the highway. What did this pattern mean for the future of his company? Not breakthrough performance. A company requires a talented team to reach its full potential. Unless Max became willing to shift his command-and-control approach, he wasn't going to be able to build that dream team.

Times are always changing, and leaders must be willing to change too. Just look at the Great Resignation. Some of this might be generational, but it's also people of all ages reassessing their lives as a result of the global pandemic.

Change can be uncomfortable, but it's not optional.

Charles Darwin famously said, "It is not the strongest of the species that survive, nor the most intelligent, but the one most responsive to change." If you want to lead a breakthrough organizational culture, you must be continuously learning and evolving. This requires a growth mindset rather than the type of fixed mindset that Max was stuck in.

Personal Accountability

Personal accountability is the capacity to take responsibility for one's own actions, obligations, and decisions without excuses. This sounds simple, but we've all seen, and perhaps even participated in, the blame game. "It's not my fault!" we plead, playing the victim. People with low personal accountability are afraid of the repercussions they might face if they admit a mistake or failure. Those who struggle with personal accountability are often not trusted by their peers, management, and those who report to them. Clearly, this would not be ideal for anyone in a leadership position, much less the CEO of a company.

A person who has a strong sense of personal accountability owns up to their results—both the good and the bad. They don't make excuses for bad decisions, failures, or mistakes. Instead, they make every effort to correct the problem and learn from the experience. A person with a poor sense of personal accountability seeks to place blame elsewhere. Either the world is against them or some outside force or person caused the problem—never them. These types of people often have a fragile sense of self-worth and fear detracting from their own self-image. They're more focused on protecting their image than overcoming challenges in order to achieve the goal at hand.

Clearly, personal accountability must be modeled by not only an organization's leadership team but anyone who oversees direct reports. The more people practicing personal accountability in an organization, the more innovative and growth oriented it can become. When individuals hold themselves accountable, they build trust among colleagues and lubricate the wheels of the engine. Doing so eliminates friction and allows people and teams to move more quickly and fluidly through problems and challenges. This encourages innovation and growth. Make sure that, as the CEO, you are practicing personal accountability and find ways to encourage it throughout your organization.

What Is a Growth Mindset?

Stanford University psychologist Carol Dweck coined the terms "fixed mindset" and "growth mindset" in her 2007 book *Mindset: The New Psychology of Success.* These mindsets, she wrote, describe people's underlying beliefs about learning and intelligence. Those with a fixed mindset believe that a person's abilities, intelligence, and talents are innate or fixed traits. Those with a growth mindset believe a person's abilities, intelligence, and talents can be enriched through continuous training, learning, and practice. Individuals typically aren't aware of which mindset they have, but Dweck's research showed that behaviors are a strong indicator of a person's mindset, especially when it comes to challenges and failure.

People with a fixed mindset, Dweck found, tend to put in minimal effort. They give up easily when faced with an obstacle. Those with a growth mindset, on the other hand, see challenges as an opportunity to problem-solve and failure as an opportunity to learn. They're continually working to improve. They're open to new ideas and new ways of doing things.

How does a growth mindset drive business? Well, for one thing, research shows that managers see far more leadership potential in their employees when a company adopts a growth mindset. Microsoft is demonstrating the truth of this research every day. Over the past few years, the forty-year-old software giant, led by CEO Satya Nadella, has adopted a growth-mindset approach to shaping its culture and developing its people. Increasingly, they are embracing Walt Disney's famous philosophy: "If you can dream it, you can do it." The company has adopted a number of initiatives to foster a growth-mindset culture. The results, though still early, are already impressive:

> By giving many more people chances to become leaders, these programs are unleashing greater potential across the company, and may well be instrumental in attracting new people. While Microsoft is still in the early phases of adopting a growth mindset throughout the organization, this cultural component can't be overstated. The company is already seeing the benefits in the form of more-innovative ideas and products—and employees are developing leadership skills in unexpected places, at every level.

Other major companies, such as General Electric, Bloomberg, Procter and Gamble, and Apple, are also adopting a growth-mindset approach to culture. But growth-mindset cultures don't just bubble up. Contrast Max's journey to Nadella's journey at Microsoft and you'll see how growth-mindset cultures die or thrive based on the beliefs that filter down from the CEO and executive team. A company and its leadership team can't fake a growth-mindset culture. As the CEO, you must embody it. This is the commitment you'll be making: "Whatever there is to learn, whatever challenges I face, I will lean in with a beginner's mind and see what I need to see, learn what I need to learn, and hear what I need to hear so I can be who I was meant to be." If you have a growth mindset, you . . .

- like to try new things.
- see failure and challenges as an opportunity to grow.
- can learn to do anything.
- are collaborative and appreciative of others' ideas and perspectives.
- are inspired by the success of others.

On the flip side, we all know people in powerful positions who have an overactive ego. We discussed this in chapters one and two. They say no often. They yell when things go wrong. They don't listen. They're closed to new ideas. They don't delegate. They don't trust others. They're jealous of other people's success. They build emotional walls. They're grumpy and ungrateful. This is what a fixed mindset looks like.

No one just wakes up one day and starts behaving like a jerk. It takes many, many years for these types of negative behaviors to emerge, settle in, and become fixed patterns. As discussed in earlier chapters, these behaviors are our subconscious's way of protecting us from pain and fear—often in response to childhood experiences that made us afraid or sad. If you are exhibiting *any* of these traits, go back and do the necessary personal work to grow beyond these obstacles. Start as soon as possible, because this work could be challenging and takes time. You won't be ready to build a growth-mindset culture until you have a handle on your own emotions and behaviors. If you want breakthrough success for yourself and your company, this work isn't optional. As Gandhi said, "You must be the change you wish to see in the world."

GROWTH, WE CAN!
I CAN! How can I?
What is possible? I will find a way!
I MAY NEED TO SHIFT.
I need to get curious. I am in control
I AM NOT MY   of my thoughts.
THOUGHTS. I am not my past.
I may have some beliefs that are
limiting myself and my potential.
I AM A CREATOR.
I try new things for fun.
I enjoy stretch
  projects.

I REACT.
You made me.
After all I have been through.
It is your fault.   WHY ME?
If they would just......
THIS AGAIN? It will never work.
If it were not for these people.......
MY PAST DETERMINES MY FUTURE.
CHANGE IS SO HARD.
I am a reactor.
I KNOW THAT
ALREADY.

Preparing for the Growth Journey

It's time for some self-care. This isn't some soft personal recommendation from me—it's science. Your brain needs certain chemicals called neurotransmitters to create an environment for neural change. You see, in moving from a fixed to a growth mindset, you are actually rewiring your brain.

If you have a fixed mindset, your brain is probably lacking in the four main chemicals responsible for feelings of happiness: dopamine, serotonin, endorphins, and oxytocin. Increasing the levels of these chemicals in your brain will lay the groundwork for increased neuroplasticity—the brain's ability to form and reorganize synaptic connections, especially in response to learning or new experiences. How do you increase the level of these chemicals and thus create an optimal neural environment for growth and change? Science tells us simple self-care can make a big difference.

1. **Get more and better-quality sleep.** There is so much science on how this improves quality of life and brain function.
2. **Improve your diet.** Eat fewer foods with preservatives and high sugar. Eat more fruits, vegetables, and complex grains. More and more science is demonstrating the powerful connection between a healthy gut and a healthy brain.
3. **Exercise more.** Movement oxygenates the body and awakens the mighty mitochondria, known as the powerhouse of the human cell.
4. **Train your brain to focus.** Meditation and concentrating on simple tasks can help. Stop multitasking. Take a break from technology.
5. **Calm your brain.** Engage in quiet, mindful activities like taking a walk in the woods.
6. **Do new things.** Take music lessons. Craft. Learn to fly fish. A brain that's learning is a brain that's growing.

7. **Practice gratitude.** Did you know that, when we express gratitude, our brain releases dopamine and serotonin? Amazing, right?

8. **Engage in deep observation.** Learn to use all your senses in order to more fully experience the world around you. Stop and smell the roses—literally.

If this all still sounds froufrou to you, then you definitely have a fixed mindset. And, like my friend Max, you don't even know you're exhibiting the traits of a fixed mindset. Max was tired, angry, and frustrated. He didn't see his high turnover rate as an opportunity to grow and learn. It was just a problem that he wanted to go away. He had no idea that his fixed mindset was the real problem. Remember, research shows that most of us aren't self-aware—in fact, we're not even aware that we lack self-awareness. Many of us suffer from unconscious incompetence, which we explored in chapter one. If most of the suggested changes above make you feel uncomfortable, it's a good indicator you need to start doing *all* of these things as soon as possible.

In addition to self-care, we've already talked about taking an honest look in the mirror. In the beginning, though, there's a lot you probably won't be able to see because you don't yet have sufficient self-awareness. What can help is some honest external feedback from friends, family, and professional colleagues. This starts with asking important questions in an environment of trust and deep listening. You're probably not going to like some of the answers you hear—but keep listening. Don't let an overactive ego put you on the defensive. You'll likely be surprised by what you learn about yourself and how others see you. Be open to this important phase of the journey to a growth mindset. You have to get out of your comfort zone to learn, adapt, and evolve.

Open your mind, your heart, and your will, and let's do some deep listening. In the last chapter, we discussed the five types of listening. They cover *how* we listen. But there are also four levels of listening. These explore *why* we listen and the prism through which we interpret what we actually hear in our interactions with others—our capacity to fully absorb the wisdom that is being shared. As a leader, it's important to try to master the highest level of listening. This won't happen overnight. In fact, it may take a lifetime, but that's okay. As you work on self-care and addressing all that emotional, reactive baggage you're carrying around from the past, the how and why of your listening will evolve. You'll begin to hear things differently. It's all interconnected, and you're headed in the right direction.

Level 1: Listening from Habits. In the status quo, for most conversations, you walk into the room with a lot of baggage—all those preconceived notions you have about the person to whom you're talking. Since you're out of your comfort zone, all of your defense mechanisms will also be shouting in your brain—stay superficial; don't go deep and make yourself vulnerable as a leader! It won't be easy to truly hear what the person is saying if you're allowing your brain to download all these previous judgements and old opinions. *Quiet the noise in your head. Lean in and listen like you're hearing this person speak for the very first time.*

Level 2: Listening from Outside. As you learn to quiet your mind, you'll start hearing new ideas, facts, and data that challenge some of your own assumptions. This is a good indicator that your listening skills are improving. You're probably still trying to shake off old habits, but you're opening your mind to what the person in front of you is sharing. This means you're becoming more self-aware. *Keep up the good work. Lean in further. Let down your barriers and open your heart to the person in front of you.*

Level 3: Listening from Within. When a conversation not only challenges your assumptions but also allows you to see reality through another person's perspective, you're making significant progress. To see yourself through the experience of another human is the foundation of empathetic listening. You are now listening with your mind *and* your heart. This means you're hearing so much more than data points and facts; you're experiencing a whole new perspective. There's an emotional connection between you and the speaker. *To master the fourth level of listening, you must leave your fears behind and make yourself vulnerable. You must intentionally lean in and value the experience of learning from others.*

Level 4: Listening from Spirit/Source/Infinite Intelligence. A level-four conversation is transformative. These conversations give birth to breakthrough ideas and profound innovation. Everyone is fully present and listening in the spirit of collaboration, trust, and respect. The energy generated by these conversations is palpable. It's generative. Everyone in the room feels that energy, and it feels great! No challenge is too big and no idea too small. *If you're able to listen from your highest level of consciousness and tap into the collective intelligence in the room, you've clearly done the personal work necessary to lead yourself and others. You can also replicate an environment where level-four listening can occur. This will change everything for you and your team.*

Congratulations! You're taking care of your intellect, emotions, body, and spirit. You're becoming more self-aware and creating a neural environment that is primed for growth. You're listening more deeply and learning from others—and you're even enjoying it. All of this creates a strong foundation for a growth mindset. Now you're ready for the next step: paving the way for breakthrough performance for you and your executive team.

KEY TAKEAWAYS

- Adopt a growth mindset and work intentionally to avoid behavior and language associated with a fixed mindset.
- Practice self-care to prepare for the growth ahead. Take care of your mind, body, and spirit.
- Become aware of how you listen and master the higher levels of deep listening.

BRAINHACK

Daily exercise is important, but running five miles a day isn't for everyone. Exercises don't have to be something long and grueling. Did you know that, on average, walking a mile burns almost the same number of calories as running one does? Daily exercise can simply be going for a walk, stretching for ten minutes, or doing a short twenty-minute exercise video. The most important thing is that you're circling blood through your body and MOVING. Your brain's motto is use it or lose it. The less you move, the harder it'll become to do so. Create a movement practice that is realistic and that you can commit to and make a habit. A healthy body is one that is in motion.

POWERFUL QUESTIONS

- What is resonating for you in this chapter?
- When it comes to your own growth, which area of self-care would benefit most from your attention?
- What three actions could you take to improve your personal well-being?

CHAPTER 6

Paving the Way for Breakthrough Performance

"A breakthrough occurs when you recognize you are more energy than matter."

—— CAROLINE MYSS ——

id you know fleas can jump one hundred fifty times their body height? It's a skill that helps them survive. But they're also very easy to train. A famous experiment placed fleas in a jar with the lid closed for three days. When the lid was taken off, the fleas stayed in the jar. They never jumped higher than the lid—even when the lid was no longer there. They were trapped in the jar forever, even though there was an easy way to escape and be free. This self-limiting behavior was now set for the rest of their lives. And, when these fleas reproduced, their offspring would automatically adhere to this same limitation. Their children would also be unnecessarily trapped by their parents' self-limiting behavior.

Contrast this with humanity's mission to go to the moon. On May 25, 1961, President John F. Kennedy stood before Congress and said that the US should commit itself to achieving this goal before the end of the decade. A year later, he would inspire the nation again with this vision as the Apollo project began in earnest. "We choose to go to the moon in this decade and do the other things," Kennedy stated, "not because they are easy, but because they are hard." Kennedy was a persuasive speaker, but, at the time, he had very little scientific evidence to support his vision or demonstrate to the public his goal was achievable. In fact, a 1961 Gallup poll indicated that 58 percent of Americans were opposed to Kennedy's idea. Despite these obstacles, Apollo 11 Commander Neil Armstrong climbed down the ladder on July 20, 1969 and walked on the moon. With more than half a billion people watching on television, Armstrong said the famous words that now grace every American history textbook: "That's one small step for a man, one giant leap for mankind."

Study the history of major breakthroughs—in performance, culture, sports, business, science, or elsewhere—and you'll see common themes and characteristics. Foundationally, what you'll never see are self-limiting behaviors (fleas), and what you'll always see is vision and an inspiring articulation of that vision (Kennedy). If you want to bust a hole in the current state, mitigate the power of self-limiting behaviors on your mood and behaviors and start living your vision. How do you begin? Well, first you have to get honest about everything that's in the way, everything that's holding you back—and you have to start with yourself, not others. Are you acting like a flea or JFK? Do you wake up every morning plagued by self-doubt and fear? Or have you committed to a vision that you're willing to work toward every day? The more personal development you have done to strengthen your higher self and align your thoughts and behaviors with your personal values and vision, the more likely you are to experience personal and professional breakthroughs.

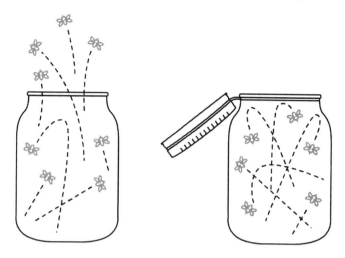

What Is a Breakthrough?

A breakthrough is an exponential jump in what's possible. As a leader, you have to see what you can't see so you can be what you want to be. Once you can see it, you must align your thoughts and actions with that vision. As I've said numerous times, all of this must happen in your own life before you can inspire your executive team and others to commit to a shared vision. It's okay if you're not ready yet. Just keep doing the work you need to do. If you focus on improving yourself, you'll get to where you need to be. When you feel you're ready to transition from the individual work you're doing now (which must be ongoing) to teamwork with your fellow leaders, here are some actions that will help you build a solid foundation for the transition:

Declare Your Vision

We've talked a lot about vision in this book. It's time to declare yours. Make an unbendable commitment to what shall be—like JFK did. Embrace your vision and clear away everything that's in the way.

Start with a clean slate. You must live in alignment with the person you've declared yourself to be and the vision you've committed to making a reality. Take all those broken agreements, disappointments, failures, and other garbage from your past and call them learning experiences—water under the bridge. When you release the grip of self-limiting beliefs and behaviors that have held you back, there is wisdom in those moments. As I've mentioned in earlier chapters, our brains are wired to remember failures, to be hesitant to break through limits, and to be fearful of what we don't know. To overcome this, you must put a firm stake in the ground and make an irrevocable shift in your thinking and behavior. Everything you do must be aligned with who you say you are and what you've committed to do in order to achieve your vision. This is the moment when everything changes forever. Declare it!

Hold Yourself Accountable

Once you've declared your vision and committed to it, you must hold yourself accountable. This is central to your success. You can't let yourself off the hook. You can't sell out. You can't revert to old behaviors, patterns, and negative thoughts. I'll say it again: you must live in alignment with the person you've declared yourself to be and the vision you've committed to making a reality. This means you're walking the talk and embodying your values, mission, and vision every hour of every day. No excuses. Anything short of this will hinder your ability to break through. How does this look in the real world? Well, for example, if you declare that part of your vision is to create a more diverse and inclusive company, but the only people helping you make decisions look and think exactly like you, then your behavior and your vision are not in alignment. Hold yourself accountable and fix that problem immediately and for good.

Maintain Integrity

Did you know that integrity means more than being incorruptible? It's also defined as the quality or state of being complete or undivided. In other words, you can't live in a state of integrity and be at war with yourself. This comes right back to the statement I made earlier: you must live in alignment with the person you've declared yourself to be and the vision you've committed to making a reality. When the going gets tough—and you know there will be those days—you can't just put your values, mission, and vision on the shelf for twenty-four hours. You must steady yourself and stay the course. If you can't trust yourself, why should others trust you? Additionally, if you look in the mirror and see someone who lacks integrity, you'll lose self-esteem and self-respect. You will be tested, and your ego's evolutionary wiring will undermine your efforts every step of the way. It'll remind you of your limitations and all the bad things that are most certainly hanging right around the corner. Some days it'll feel like three steps forward and two steps back. You've got to exercise grit and determination to stay on course for your personal transformation.

Up to this point in the book, you've been working on yourself. This was the right place to start—the only place to start. Now, you need to bring everything you've learned to your executive team and inspire them to do this same deep work—first as individuals, then as a group. Remember, you're building a new organizational culture from the inside out because that's the only way to create real and sustainable change. How are you going to convince others to do the work that you've done? Undoubtedly, they've watched your behavior improve over the last few months as you've become more self-aware and started to live in alignment with your values and vision. The next phase of your journey will be learning to express all this to others, to help your executive team understand why the work you've done is important, meaningful, and worthy of their attention. We're talking about moving from personal alignment to group alignment, and that means mastering a new skill: communication. Communication is everything when it comes to inspiring breakthrough performance.

The Four Culture Quadrants

Many leaders want an ideal, high-performance culture but don't know how to create a work atmosphere where their people can operate as their highest and best selves. For people to be able to self-actualize, the organization must have a high-challenge, high-support environment. No one is bored or overwhelmed in such an environment because they're asked to push beyond their comfort zone—which leads to personal and professional growth—while being fully supported by their colleagues and bosses.

But most companies don't operate in the high-challenge, high-support quadrant. More commonly, companies have high-challenge environments with little support or, even worse, no challenge and no support—both of which lead to stress, a lack of fulfillment, and ultimately burnout. Here are the four quadrants from Aaron Schmookler, co-founder, trainer, and "culture engineer" at Yes Works:

1. Performance Catalyst: an "always improving" culture—high challenge/high support

2. Status Quo: a "how we've always done it" culture—low challenge/high support
3. Depressive Dead Zone: an "entropy-rules" culture—no challenge/no support
4. Fear and Self Protection: a "manipulation, avoidance, self-interested" culture—high challenge/low support

Unfortunately, many organizations unconsciously or unintentionally create low-challenge, low-support environments. This leads to the opposite of a high-performance culture—an environment where no one gets out of their comfort zone. People are coddled, not challenged. You can't achieve high performance if your company is operating in this quadrant. So, what quadrant is your company operating in?

There are two sides to all communication—internal and external. With internal communication, or self-talk, we've already discussed that the majority of our thoughts are negative. You'll have to work intentionally to combat negative thoughts and replace them with positive self-talk. You don't want to fall back into old habits as you transition to the next phase of igniting your company's culture. There's too much at stake. If you tell yourself that you can't achieve something, that will come true, and you'll never achieve it. If, on the other hand, you remind yourself every day that you're capable of turning your vision into a reality, then so it shall be. Breakthrough performance requires positive self-talk. Become cognizant of your self-talk and make sure it's fortifying your vision and values, not diminishing them.

External communication—what you say to others—is equally important. Some of the biggest problems leaders face are lack of buy-in and an absence in ownership. As you prepare to move from the internal work you're doing as an individual to the external work of inspiring your executive team, you're going to need to learn what inspires change. Your choice of words must become very intentional.

In their bestselling book *The Three Laws of Performance*, authors Steve Zaffron and Dave Logan state the simple, universal principles that drive breakthrough performance:

1. **How people perform correlates to how situations occur to them.** This is about people's beliefs and how they see any given situation. If people believe a situation is unchangeable, they'll act as if the situation is unchangeable. Think fleas. If they believe something can be changed, they'll act as if the situation can be changed. Our past experiences shape our assumptions, hopes, fears, and beliefs. In turn, these shape our behaviors and performance. As humans, we expect the future to be more of the past. That's what Zaffron and Logan call the "default future." Stop and think about the importance of that for a moment. If someone's past has been filled with disappointment, abuse, or tragedy, that's their default future. As a leader, you must recognize this powerful force in others' beliefs and actions. The only way that you as a leader can help them rewrite their default future is to help them recognize their past doesn't have to be their future. You're most likely going to need some professional expertise to do this. It's also going to take a lot of deep listening on your part. Hopefully, you've made significant progress on your listening skills. Most corporate initiatives backfire because they fail to acknowledge and change people's perceptions and, as a result, their performance. Your company can't break through without addressing the reality stated in this first principle.

2. **How a situation occurs arises in language.** Language has a profound impact on our thoughts and behaviors. In America, we greet each other by asking, "How are you?" In some countries, where survival is especially challenging, people open conversations by asking, "Nothing bad?" The choice of words and implied difference in tone is striking, even in

these short phrases. We use language to share our beliefs and life experiences. Most of us have developed strong patterns of communication as a result of our experiences. We have specific body language and words and phrases we like to use—many of them are negative and unconstructive. If you want others to buy into the future you envision, you must align your communication style with your vision and help others become more aware of their communication patterns. Again, this will take a lot of deep listening and undoubtedly some training to help yourself and others communicate more effectively and constructively. Remember, companies are human systems, so this is the only way to help your company let go of its default future and embrace a new, shared vision.

3. **Future-based language transforms how situations occur to people.** When JFK spoke about sending someone to the moon, he transformed what most people thought was possible. To rewrite the future of your company, you must shift people's perceptions from what has happened in the past to what can be in the future. Zaffron and Logan say that "leaders listen for the future of their organizations." As leaders move people from a default future toward a new vision, they must start with a blank page and create the necessary space and processes to allow everyone in the company to explore, debate, and coauthor the future. This creates engagement, a foundational step toward ownership. You can't incentivize your way to a vision. It will backfire. People must make the vision their own. They must understand how the vision aligns with their own values and purpose. This is the only way that your vision can become a shared vision. This is how buy-in and ownership unfold and amazing breakthroughs happen. When your employees are intrinsically motivated, working cohesively through shared values, and inspired by the mission of your organization, magic happens.

One thread that runs through all three of these principles is listening. It's a skill I've emphasized in numerous chapters. Its value can't be overstated. In an interview about their book, Zaffron and Logan said it best:

> The fundamental aspect of leadership that most people miss is the importance of listening. Listening, as we describe it, is not simply gathering data and opinions from people, but rather exploring how situations occur to them, what they aspire to make happen, and what stands in their way. By listening in this way, leaders combine what they hear from lots of people into an invented future that represents the bulk of people's concerns. When people hear the invented future, they say, "That speaks for me!" because it is, in part, their idea. Lack of buy-in and ownership are replaced with excitement, inspired action, and full engagement.

Are you ready for the next phase of your journey? Are you ready to work with your executive team to shape a new future? If you've done the important personal work necessary to embody the change you want to see, then you're ready. Remember, you are the foundation for what comes next. With an open heart and mind, it's time to start working with your executive team so they can begin their personal journeys of change and growth. You've examined and shaken off what has been holding you back. Now it's time to help others do the same. By helping the individuals on your executive team develop themselves, you will strengthen the humans and the human systems that comprise your company. In sharing your vision while listening to theirs, you will create a shared vision together. You'll listen more deeply and communicate more constructively. A bond of trust and an atmosphere of respect and collaboration will be formed. The way others listen and communicate will evolve as well. Let the alignment begin!

KEY TAKEAWAYS

- As a leader, you must see what you can't see so you can be who you want to be. Once you can see it, align your thoughts and actions with that vision.
- Declare your vision, hold yourself accountable, and maintain integrity.
- Study and understand Steve Zaffron and Dave Logan's *The Three Laws of Performance*.

BRAINHACK

One of the easiest ways to change your brain and practice self-care is through positive affirmations. By constantly repeating empowering phrases, you can change the neuropathways in your brain. The more focus and attention you give to the pathways that produce positive thoughts, feelings, and emotions in your brain, the stronger they will become, and less energy will be put towards the pathways producing negative emotions like anger, fear, or depression. Write some positive phrases on sticky notes and place them on your bathroom mirror. Every morning, when you get ready, repeat them in your head or out loud. The more you repeat them, the stronger the neural pathways will become.

POWERFUL QUESTIONS

- What is resonating for you in this chapter?
- Have you shared your vision for the enterprise in a way that your leadership team understands and sees themselves executing as leaders?
- Is your level of rigor in discipline at the level it needs to be to accomplish what is needed for your company to be a Market Leader?

If you want to take your learning journey to the next level, I have created a series of trainings that support you in, deepening your learning while equipping you in getting into action to cultivate the kind of culture required to be a market leader.

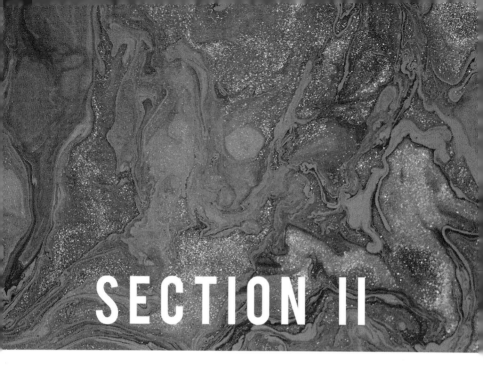

SECTION II

The Leadership Team

Is It Impaired or Inspired?

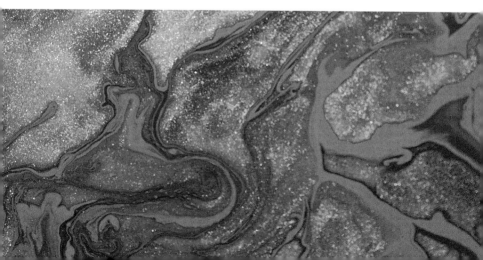

CHAPTER 7

What Got You Here Isn't Enough to Break Through

"Blind to the transparency of our actions, we confuse the image we want to project with the being we want to bring forth."

HUMBERTO MATURANA,
—— AUTHOR OF THE TREE OF KNOWLEDGE ——

U p to this point, everything I've recommended has been about you, the top leader of your organization. This is as it should be. Maybe you feel like Atlas, the Titan in Greek mythology who was forced to hold the world on his shoulders. After all, you do shoulder a lot of responsibility. People count on you every day. There's no doubt that it can be exhausting, which is why you need to be mentally, physically, emotionally, and spiritually fit to lead yourself before you can lead others. If you've committed to the required and ongoing work that we've discussed so far, you're now ready to prepare your executive team for the transformational change ahead. If you want to foster sustainable change, they need you and you need them. Let's face it, no matter how fit you are, you're not a mythological god. You can't hold up the world on your own. You are a single human leading a human system. Empower others and ignite the potential of the human system you're leading and, together, you can achieve anything—without all the weight you're feeling now. Not only does this set your company up for success, but it's quite liberating for you and your leadership team.

Organizational culture is shaped and determined by the behavioral norms of the leadership team and the norms that it endorses. Before changing those behavioral norms, you must recognize that everything that got you, your executive team, and your company to this moment isn't enough for the breakthrough performance you desire. Just as you devoted time to strengthening your skills as a leader, the members of your executive team must do the necessary work as individuals and as a group. This means assessing what needs to change and replacing outdated or detrimental habits with new, productive ones. A new mindset and openness to change is required by everyone on the leadership team. The reality is that not everyone will be willing to make the journey with you. Remember, our brains are wired to resist change—and resist some will. But, for those open to the personal and professional growth you're offering, this journey is about deconstructing dysfunction and replacing it with healthy, high-performance behaviors. According to the Human Synergistics® Organizational Culture Inventory by R.A. Cooke and J.C. Lafferty, it's about creating an organizational culture that promises four things:

1. Expectations for achievement through alignment around a shared company mission, values, and goals.
2. Expectations for self-actualization through a human system where people can operate at their highest level and contribute their unique skills, talents, and ideas.
3. Expectations for humanistic-encouraging behaviors where people genuinely care for, respect, and listen to one another.
4. Expectations for an affiliative environment where people can effectively share, collaborate, and innovate.

This is the ideal. This is what everyone wants. It's simple and straightforward. But why is it so elusive? Why are these promises so challenging for leaders to make and keep? Think back to the beginning of your personal leadership journey. Getting started was the toughest part, right? Becoming more self-aware and changing your thoughts and behaviors has taken practice and discipline. Change is uncomfortable, especially in the beginning. Newton's Laws of Motion explain it best: "An object at rest will stay at rest, and an object in motion will stay in motion at constant velocity, unless acted upon by an unbalanced force. Inertia is the tendency of an object to resist changes in its velocity: whether in motion or motionless." Whether we are "at rest" and need to speed up or "in motion" and need to slow down, our brains are wired to resist the switch. See, even physics is against us! To increase velocity, you and your team must become the unbalanced force. That's right: Atlas must shrug.

Progression of Change Initiatives

As your organization prepares for significant change, it's a good idea to do a reset with the executive team. State your intentions around the change effort and enroll your team in your vision. Inspire them and prepare them to accomplish the extraordinary. Here are the stages you'll need to move through as you lay the groundwork for the significant adjustments ahead.

1. **Starting Point**: In this origination stage, you shape and clearly articulate your vision for change. You also commit to outcomes, milestones, and timelines—and appoint change-leaders.

2. **Getting to Work:** During this stage, discipline, focus and intentionality are required. Building trust and keeping agreements is paramount. Grit and determination are non negotiable at this stage. There is intense and intentional heavy lifting underway.

3. **Gaining Traction:** Now, things start working. Stick to the plan. Acknowledge wins, big and small. Engage more contributors. Maintain integrity and keep agreements. Continued discipline are key in this stage. Rinse, repeat, and build momentum.

4. **Breakthrough:** You are getting to critical mass. The plan is working and people see the benefits. More people want to contribute. New ideas are generated and owned. Everyone is moving in the same direction now. Conflict is replaced by alignment, and amazing things are beginning to happen.

5. **Reliability:** You're reliably repeating your success and moving forward. Personal accountability is being practiced, and there are structures and processes in place to support specific goals. You're also regularly measuring your progress now. Humility and curiosity are important during this stage.

6. **Succession:** You're in the zone now, with strong skills, knowledge, and experience. Excellence prevails. There is delegation and replication. Continued engagement, contribution, and innovation are key in this stage.

Every initiative, improvement, or change effort has its ups and downs. So, what happens when something goes wrong? This is an operating state as well. If you lose a big client, your supply chain breaks down, or have a dismal quarter in the middle of your change effort, we call this state danger or emergency. When this happens, the leader must step in and do what needs to be done. Temporarily, this state requires the project leader to override any empowerment strategies that might have been put in place. This state is about saving people from a burning building. Once the danger or emergency has passed, the change effort can proceed.

So how do you begin?

First, you need to understand the makeup of your executive team. What is the team's DNA? What are their challenges collectively and individually? What motivates them? What personality types are at the table? What are their beliefs? How does everyone get along? How strong are the bonds of trust between them? How do they communicate? How do certain personalities empower or stifle others? What are the power dynamics on the team? What are the key behavior patterns? What is the team's decision-making style? Can you see what makes the team effective and special as well as where the gaping holes exist in the team's thinking, behaviors, and leadership competencies? It's time to *fully* understand the makeup of your leadership team. To effectively inspire and motivate them, you must understand how they think, work, interact, and make decisions together and as individuals. This will provide the necessary framework for change and growth. At my consulting firm, we use the following tools:

- Stakeholder-centered 360-degree feedback (Marshall Goldsmith)
- DISC assessments
- Myer-Briggs Type Indicator (MBTI)
- Gallup's StrengthsFinder

- Enneagram
- The IHHP emotional intelligence (EQ) quiz
- Innermetrix assessments
- Big 5
- The Achiever
- Positive Intelligence's Saboteurs Assessment
- Human Synergistics Organizational Culture Inventory/ Organizational Effectiveness Inventory (OCI®/EOI)

Data from these in-depth assessments helps my team learn what drives each person on the leadership team. It also helps us understand the group dynamics. If you know what drives people and how they perceive their world, colleagues, and work, then you know what they need to feel fulfilled and self-actualized. This is key. We also gain key insights into individual communication styles and core competencies. Once we really have a full picture of who is leading the company and how they work together, we have a strong foundation to facilitate change.

Deconstructing Dysfunction

Understanding business is like understanding life. Like people, companies go through stages of growth and maturity. Renowned entrepreneur and business/life strategist Tony Robbins describes the business lifecycle this way: at first, there is the company's birth, infancy, and toddler years; next, companies go through the teen and young adult stages; later, companies reach the zone of maximum maturity, the mid-life evaluation, the senior years, and ultimately death. Sometimes, though, along the way, companies get stuck. They stop maturing or even regress. According to the Adizes Institute, an influential global organizational development firm:

At the foundation of effective management for any organization is the fundamental truth that all organizations, like all living organisms, have a lifecycle and undergo very predictable and repetitive patterns of behavior as they grow and develop.

At each new stage of development an organization is faced with a unique set of challenges. How well or poorly management addresses these challenges and leads a healthy transition from one stage to the next, has a significant impact on the success or failure of their organization.

So, in addition to understanding your leadership team, you need to understand where your company is in that lifecycle—and whether it's growing or stuck. Unfortunately, when my team arrives to help facilitate change, the leadership team often doesn't know where the company is in its lifecycle and has no idea that the company is stuck—or sometimes even regressing. If revenue isn't growing, profitability is stagnant, the company is losing customers or employees, the same problems keep happening, or there's little or no innovation, then something is amiss. This is the time to figure out what's keeping your company from maturing. This is the time to figure out what's holding back your human system.

There's a good chance old habits and entrenched behaviors are the root cause. Through your own work as the organization's leader, you've had to unlearn certain ways of acting, communicating, and behaving in order to evolve, grow, and become a better leader. The results of that important work have prepared you to now help your executive team do the same. You started your journey by taking an honest look in the mirror. Once you understood yourself better, you could address your weaknesses and capitalize on your strengths. Then, with a clearer vision of yourself, you committed to change. You began adopting a healthier mindset and behaviors. You became more disciplined and intentional in your approach to life and work. This is what is now required of your executive team.

Awareness is the foundation of all meaningful change and growth. But recall from the research I've shared in previous chapters that awareness doesn't come easily to humans or human systems. Subconsciously, we tell ourselves, "Why look too deeply? Everything is fine. We've been doing it like this forever. It's all good." In its endless quest to protect us from the new and unknown, our brain—particularly our ego—makes it easy for us to say everything is fine, even when it's not. Hearing the word "fine" sets off alarm bells for me. It's not a word associated with breakthrough or high-performance organizations. Just because an activity, behavior, or pattern feels fine doesn't mean it is right. Ingrained habits can trick us into thinking everything is good, even if the world is falling apart around us. That's how badly the human brain clings to the status quo in order to avoid change. But, if your organization is stuck or regressing, change isn't optional.

Take Cali Stonebridge's successful Atlanta architecture business, which hit $25 million in revenue last year. The firm should have been pushing through the expected challenges of the teen/young-adult lifecycle phase, but instead it was toddling through a labyrinth of problems that smaller, younger companies often navigate. Cali and her team had been so busy growing and doing the work that they had overlooked many of the foundational steps necessary to grow a strong team and culture. Even at this stage in the company's lifecycle, Cali was still the head architect, CEO, head of sales, and main point of contact for all premier clients. She was playing Atlas, and the burden was no longer sustainable.

When we were invited in to assess her team and company culture, we immediately saw the problem. All eight members of her executive team were motivated by one thing: design. Their work was stellar, steady, and conscientious but lacked processes and structure. Managing stress, which is a natural part of growth, was also a big challenge for all of them. Infrastructure was lacking, and no one was in charge of building it. In fact, no one was even interested in building infrastructure because they were so focused on the creative aspect of their work. Everything that had brought them to the current level of success—all their good design work—couldn't help them break through to the next phase of growth. The company was a teenager behaving like a toddler, which is never good. Too much time was being spent managing frustrated clients who loved the firm's design work but not the missed deadlines and cost overruns. Internally, every couple of years, a few architects would leave because they found the job too stressful. They walked out the door complaining about a lack of support and training. Cali was a talented architect who had hired other talented architects. She had *not* hired any process-oriented people to help run and grow her business. The company's executive team was homogenous. It lacked balance. Everyone was motivated by the same thing. As a result, her company was stuck—and possibly beginning to regress. Until we showed her the problem, she didn't even realize that operational management was critical to scaling her firm. She had a blind spot that was unhinging her company.

Cali isn't alone. In fact, 75 percent of the businesses I consult lack what I call "organizational awareness" and have at least one critical blind spot. When we go into a company, not only do we uncover missing competencies around important business functions, but we frequently discover that *no one has even identified or noticed that these competencies are missing*. No matter how many times my team and I experience this, we're still surprised. Everyone is walking around saying, "Everything is fine," when the organization is actually stuck or in trouble—sometimes big trouble. At Cali's firm, everyone was so busy doing what they had always done—being creative—that no one had stepped back to take an honest look at what might be causing their inability to break through to the next level of growth. As we worked with Cali, the first ah-ha moment was recognition of her blind spot around the imbalanced makeup of her executive team. Not only did she need to hire more process-oriented people, but she had to get a talented bunch of creatives to respect the importance of process and infrastructure. She and her team needed some serious professional development in this area. Otherwise, the firm would keep toddling along, putting out fires, and staying stuck as a teen behaving as a toddler. The human system Cali was leading needed to be awakened to become more self-aware and align itself around important company goals, a clear vision, and new priorities. Luckily, she and her team were willing to do the necessary work and were able to turn things around fairly quickly.

Halfway through our thirty-six-month engagement with Cali and her firm, she asked me, "How could I have been so blind to such a huge problem? I still can't quite come to terms with it." I was able to comfort her with the knowledge that blind spots and operational dysfunction were problems my team saw every day in our line of work. "Why is that?" she asked. "Dismantling dysfunctions requires awareness of those dysfunctions," I replied. "But many leaders are too busy and stressed out to see what's happening right in front of them. They don't make the time to step back and assess, and their brains try to protect them from jarring realities that will stress them out even further. It's a vicious cycle but is actually the norm, not the exception. Leaders would rather defend mediocrity than face problems and make necessary changes. When my team comes in and points out a problem, our intention is simply to see the current state clearly, figure out where the leader wants and needs to go, and help them fix anything in the way. It's pretty straightforward. But people get defensive. They take things personally. For some leaders, their whole identity is tied up in their business. In such cases, emotions often cloud reality. This is why CEOs need to work on themselves before they start working with their teams. They've got to break their own dangerous patterns before they can help others. You were willing to do the work as an individual and with your team, Cali, and that has made all the difference. Kudos to you."

Let's take a look at some of the problems a CEO can face when he or she starts to work with their executive team. Once a team dysfunction or imbalance is identified, it can usually be fixed; it's the diagnosis that can be tricky. So, here are the top six culprits I see on a fairly regular basis:

1. **Silo Mentality**—hoarding information as an individual or a team and failing to share it with others. This stifles collaboration and innovation and damages an organization's efficiency and culture.

2. **Fiefdom Syndrome**—becoming fixated on one's own activities, territory, or success to the detriment of others. The term was coined by Robert Herbold, who was COO at Microsoft back in the 1990s, and it was killing the company. Of course, this was well before Satya Nadella was named CEO there and turned things around.

3. **Win-Lose Mindset**—approaching communications with an "I'm right, you're wrong" mindset. This creates a zero-sum environment for everyone. It's a communication and innovation killer.

4. **Passive-Aggressive Behavior**—harboring negative feelings but, rather than addressing them directly, masking ill will through indirect hostilities. This type of behavior negatively impacts morale and productivity.

5. **Perfectionism**—controlling and micromanaging everything. Perfectionism is referred to as the enemy of success because it often stalls forward motion.

6. **Cordial Hypocrisy**—in their book *Building Trust*, authors Robert C. Solomon and Fernando Flores define this as "the strong tendency of people in organizations, because of loyalty or fear, to pretend that there is trust when there is none, to be polite in the name of harmony when cynicism and distrust are active poisons, eating away at the very existence of the organization."

7. **Systemic Distrust**—organizations either have a culture of trust or distrust. When the majority of the people in an organization simply don't trust the people for and with whom they work, it's called systemic distrust. According to one PwC's global CEO survey, 55 percent of CEOs think a lack of trust is a threat to their organization's growth.

When my team works with companies, we address these entrenched behaviors in what we call deep alignment sessions, in which we:

- Identify and assess the team's current behavioral norms, patterns, and competencies.
- Address distrust between leadership team members
- Create alliances to foster effective communication and problem solving.
- Identify constraints that are impeding the team's potential for positive change and growth.
- Foster extreme ownership among all team members.
- Create a powerful new environment where effective and sustainable change and growth can happen quickly.

In these powerful, experiential, multi-day immersion workshops, leadership teams learn new ways to communicate, operate, and innovate. It's a complete recalibration in order to say goodbye to old dysfunctions and pave the way for ongoing breakthroughs. The goal is to open the hearts and minds of everyone on the leadership team so they can fully comprehend what is needed to help the organization's human system fulfill its purpose and reach its full potential. It is a crucial step in preparing an organization for sustainable transformational change. Some of the key topics we cover are active listening and effective communication, building trust, awareness of blind spots, response agility, Liberating Structures, the clean-slate approach, adapting and recalibrating, effective problem solving, and how to invent an inspiring future. After a deep alignment, the leadership team understands how they view themselves as a human system—usually for the very first time. They understand why they must change and have acknowledged that what got them to their current stage in the organization's lifecycle isn't enough to create the high-performance culture they desire now. A strong new foundation has been built, and the executive team is now primed for the next step in their transformation.

KEY TAKEAWAYS

- Organizational culture is shaped and determined by the behavioral norms of the leadership team.
- Addressing mistrust is the only path to building authentic trust.
- As the CEO, you must fully understand the makeup of your leadership team—how they think, work, interact, and make decisions together and as individuals. This will provide the necessary framework for change and growth.
- Self-awareness and organizational awareness are the foundations of all meaningful change and growth.

BRAINHACK

If you are stuck in a routine, your brain will start to use the same neural pathways repeatedly, and the rest of the pathways you aren't using will start to deteriorate. This makes it more difficult to see anything outside of the world you've created for yourself. Novelty will allow your brain to exercise existing pathways and create new ones that will take attention away from the fixed mindset you've found yourself in. Take a new route to work, use your non-dominant hand to control the mouse on your computer, sit in a new seat, and use a different-colored pen. Make small changes every day that create new experiences in your brain. Slowly, those small changes will become big changes, and your mindset will grow.

POWERFUL QUESTIONS

- What is resonating for you in this chapter?
- What old habits or entrenched behaviors might be holding you, your team, and your company back?
- How deeply aligned around a shared noble cause, organizational values, and behaviors is your leadership team?

CHAPTER 8

Alignment Is the Key to Sustainability

"Every time you are tempted to react in the same old way, ask if you want to be a prisoner of the past or a pioneer of the future."

— DEEPAK CHOPRA —

I f you and your leadership team have done the necessary work to recognize and address your personal and group issues, it's time to start building a framework for cultural transformation for your entire organization. But take note: building a framework should *never* go before the work of deep alignment that we discussed in the last chapter. If it does, you're building a house of cards. There are no shortcuts. Do these steps in the right order. It's crucial for success.

Just as you were willing to do work as an individual before helping your executive team, so must the executive team be willing to do foundational work *before* creating a change framework for the rest of the organization. According to the *Harvard Business Review*, 80 percent of cultural transformations fail—80 percent! All too often, leadership teams put the entire company through the motions of change but fail to keep their agreements. This might not be intentional. They might not even see the breakdown because they lack the necessary self- and organizational awareness. Everyone on the leadership team needs on-going personal and professional training and support in a variety of areas to support sustainable change. The first time a promise is broken, trust is broken—and, without trust, it's nearly impossible to sustain meaningful change. My intention in sharing this is not to be harsh; it's just how human systems work—from the inside out. You and your leadership team are the heart of your organization, and the heart needs to be in top condition to pump blood into the whole of the organization, especially as you take on the marathon effort required by this type of change. Stamina is essential, and stamina comes from rigorous training. This isn't optional; it's key to your success.

Over time, broken agreements have tremendous negative ripple effects in an organization. People's belief that agreements will be honored is foundational for meaningful and sustainable change. Just like you can't frame a solid house on top of a weak foundation, you can't build a strong organizational culture on top of a bunch of problems and broken agreements. Both will collapse under the slightest pressure. Do the personal work as a CEO and go through a deep alignment process as an executive team. Eliminate any VUCA—volatility, uncertainty, chaos, and ambiguity—among yourselves first. Only then will you and your team be ready to move into this new phase. I've seen the aftermath when a leadership team tries to skip the foundational work. It ain't pretty!

Types of Trust

Trust is the lynchpin for culture. There is no better resource on this topic than *Building Trust* by Fernando Flores and Robert C. Solomon, who discuss three types of trust: simple trust, blind trust, and authentic trust. Simple trust is nothing more than an unintentional habit. Blind trust is a blanket kind of trust that is offered too easily and without discernment. These first two types of "trust" are actually nothing more than misunderstandings of the important concept of authentic trust.

Most people understand the importance of trust, so it gets a lot of lip service inside organizations. But authentic trust doesn't just magically happen. It's the result of continuous attentiveness and intentional nurturing. Creating a sustainable environment of authentic trust requires personal responsibility for all members as well as organizational commitment from the leadership team and CEO. Without this, efforts to build a workplace of authentic trust are doomed. Only an environment of authentic trust provides a gateway for people and teams to experience breakthrough performance. This, in turn, contributes to a healthy, high-performance culture where people thrive.

Authentic trust should never be confused with the poisonous practice of cordial hypocrisy, which is unfortunately rampant in many corporate cultures. When people practice cordial hypocrisy, they pretend to trust what they've heard, seen, or experienced by smiling, verbally affirming, or some other outward behavior while, inside, they're hiding fear, resentment, disbelief, or some other negative emotion. They might even turn around and gossip to others about these negative feelings which breeds even more mistrust. The greatest enemies of trust are cynicism, selfishness, and a naive conception of life and work in which people expect more than they're willing to give. Resentment, distrust, and inauthenticity are the result. If cordial hypocrisy or mistrust are thriving in your organization, honest, productive communication and problem solving will be nearly impossible. It's a big problem that requires immediate attention.

Authentic trust is a matter of making and keeping commitments and telling the truth. Mistrust arises when people lose confidence in someone's ability to keep their commitments or tell the truth. Lying is always a breach of trust. When authentic trust is established between people, it transforms their relationship. Authentic trust involves sincerity, authenticity, integrity, virtue, and honor (matters of ethics). Authentic trust can never be taken for granted. It must be continuously cultivated through commitments, integrity, and truthfulness. Establish authentic trust in your organization and it will change everything! Flores and Solomon tell us that the only way to build trust is to tell the truth where there is mistrust.

Now that you and your team are deeply aligned, you're ready to create a compelling future for your organization. You may choose traditional strategic planning or follow a plan like the one mentioned in Gino Wickman's *Traction*: the "Entrepreneurs Operating System," which helps organizations create a Vision/Traction Organizer®. Or you can choose to participate in an immersive strategy session, like those my organization offers. They equip organizational leaders to create a roadmap for the company's vision, allowing them to:

- Ideate and align on the organization's noble cause as well as an inspiring, compelling, and durable mission, vision, and values.
- Agree how decisions will be made through well-defined strategic anchors.
- Align the leadership team around a thematic goal.
- Gain new perspectives on the power of accountability and integrity as a new way of being that ignites a thriving and healthy high-performance culture.

A Compelling Future always starts with a noble cause, a compelling mission, and a clear vision that are easy for both Management and employees to operationalize.

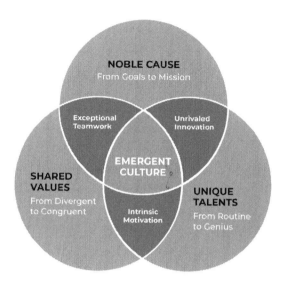

Mission Matters

As discussed in the first section of the book, you can't have a high-performance organizational culture without a noble cause. Once you define and articulate your cause or the overarching intent of the organization, it's time to define the mission, what you do day in and day out to fulfill the overarching intent. This captures how your company's core competencies make a positive impact in the world. It's what attracts the right talent to your company and encourages them to stay and fully contribute.

Making a profit isn't a noble cause. If you have to send your assistant back into the boardroom to snap a photo of your company's mission and text it to you before you speak to your team, well, your mission probably isn't shaping any positive behaviors at your organizations. Don't underestimate the power of a noble cause, especially today, when people are searching for more meaning and purpose in their work. Does your mission inspire people to want to hitch their wagons to your organization? In today's competitive talent market, a compelling noble cause and a mission that speaks to what you do and how you do it is very important.

My company's noble cause is to "forever liberate the human spirit at work." Every day, it inspires all of us. It's simple and powerful. It captures people's attention, attracting both clients and talent. We have integrated this noble cause into everything we do—from creating our program offerings, to hiring, to developing new team members. We even use it to determine which customers are best suited for our transformational work with leaders and organizations. We've already discussed how powerful causes and missions at Patagonia and Microsoft have ignited transformative change, growth, and performance at those highly successful companies. Committing to and leading in alignment with an inspiring noble cause is one of the most powerful forces for change that I've seen in my many years of helping companies build high-performance cultures.

One last note on mission: it has to be believable and aligned with the company's current core competencies. In other words, it can't be a hollow promise. I have many good and bad examples of mission statements. One of my favorite examples of a bad mission statement comes from one of the country's biggest fried-chicken chains. They promise to be a healthy choice in the fast-food world. Sorry, folks, fried chicken will never be healthy. Healthy just can't be part of a fried-chicken company's mission statement.

Values Speak Volumes

If you work for a Ritz Carlton hotel anywhere in the world, you start your day with a fifteen-minute meeting and a couple of "wow stories." These are employee stories about exceptional customer service. They're shared to reinforce the values every employee is expected to demonstrate as an ambassador of the exceptional and world-renowned Ritz-Carlton brand. At companies like this, values are . . . well . . . valued—*highly* valued. Hires, terminations, and promotions are based on an employees' alignment with the organization's values. Well-crafted values are purposeful, meaningful, and evocative. They complement the company's noble cause, mission, and shape positive behavior.

Values are ineffective when they're aspirational. They're not what an organization *hopes* to be. They articulate the company's behavior now, in its current state. Organizational-performance expert Patrick Lencioni says aspirational values are not really values at all—they're just goals. It's important to know the difference. Values build trust both within an organization and with the organization's customers and partners. When a company has clear values, it eliminates VUCA because values tell everyone in the company what's important and everyone in the world what to expect from the people who represent this company. Organization-wide commitment to a core set of values ensures that everyone delivers on the same focused set of promises. This is how influential brands like Ritz Carlton are built. Your company doesn't need a dozen values. In fact, that's too many. No one will remember them all. Microsoft has only three: accountability, integrity, and respect. These values are clear, simple, memorable, easy to understand, and straightforward to operationalize.

Strategic Anchors Promote Alignment

In his bestselling business classic, *The Advantage: Why Organizational Health Trumps Everything Else in Business*, leadership guru Patrick Lencioni coined the term "strategic anchors." It describes a simple, game-changing process for companies to answer the question "How will we succeed?" Companies that use strategic anchors have a clear competitive advantage. Whenever a question, opportunity, or problem presents itself, the executive team can quickly review the situation through the focused lens of its strategic anchors. Lencioni often uses Southwest Airlines to demonstrate how strategic anchors work. The airline has three strategic anchors: on time, low fares, and fun customer experience. These are a distillation of the company's core values down to their very essence. When an opportunity comes along, Southwest's leadership team quickly assesses whether it aligns with or compromises the organization's strategic anchors. The leadership team asks, "Will this opportunity help or hinder our ability to be on time? How will the opportunity impact our low fares? Will it enhance or detract from our fun customer experience?" If the answers to these questions reveal alignment with Southwest's strategic anchors, the leadership team moves forward. If even one of the strategic anchors is negatively impacted by the opportunity, the executive team takes a pass. Simple, right? And so liberating! This is what decision making looks like in a healthy, intentional, high-performance organization. But, most of the time, companies are asking questions like "How can we expand sales? How can we beat the competition?" These are misguided questions. The better question is "How will we succeed?" And the right answer is "by aligning everything we do with our noble cause, mission, vision and values and then assessing opportunities and threats through the focused lens of our strategic anchors." And the more humans there are in your company's human system, the more complex and bureaucratic decision making can become—all the more reason to put strategic anchors in place as early as possible.

Thematic Goals

Another Lencioni tool I value and use when facilitating a Compelling Future strategy session is thematic goals. I ask the executive team to focus on one important problem or goal for a specified amount of time, such as a month, a quarter, or a year. For example, a leadership team might commit to improving their customer-retention rate over the next six months or reversing the loss of top talent by improving its culture over this next year or reducing the cost of its deliveries this month. Interestingly, thematic goals are qualitative, not quantitative—meaning there are no specific numbers attached to the goal. They are more like a rally cry, uniting the team around a central purpose. Thematic goals encourage the executive team to sprint together towards a clear finish line. This can be very energizing. Rather than reacting to the latest business crisis, which is how many companies operate, the executive team can use thematic goals to tackle problems and embrace important opportunities *before* a crisis hits. This proactive approach is much less stressful and much more effective.

An Intentional Process

When my team met the seven members of the leadership team at Transtronic, an integrated technology company that helps bring safety to the world of travel, they had been using the popular Entrepreneurial Operating System (EOS) methodology for five years. They even had an EOS coach on staff. Unfortunately, the company had a very low success rate for accomplishing what they had set out to do. Everyone at the company was frustrated. Even the vice president of people, a member of the executive team, told me they weren't honoring their agreements or addressing problems when people failed to meet their objectives. There was little accountability and high employee turnover. Something was definitely wrong. They couldn't understand why the EOS methods weren't working. They wondered what they were doing wrong.

When the organization finally decided to work with us, we knew quickly why EOS wasn't working for them: they hadn't addressed their behavioral baggage through a deep alignment. They hadn't started with a clean slate and new way of communicating and behaving—all necessary for the type of change EOS might bring to a higher-functioning team. In other words, Transtronic had slathered EOS frosting on a mud pie—and there was no getting past the bad taste that this had left in everyone's mouths.

We conducted a deep alignment with the leadership team and worked through their many problems. Finally, they had forged the new beginning they needed to start moving forward and make sustainable changes. In fact, the leadership team was so impressed by their progress they decided to bring in the nineteen people who reported to them and go through a deep alignment immersion workshop, during which we once again helped them work on their worst entrenched behaviors: a silo mentality, fiefdom syndrome, a win-lose mindset, passive-aggressive behavior, perfectionism, and so on. To their credit, they did work through their issues, including the distrust that was plaguing every meeting and every new initiative, and committed to building trust among one another and to enacting more healthy and productive behaviors going forward.

With the deep alignment successfully completed, they finally had a strong foundation to work on a compelling future. They decided to reset their mission, vision, and values after paying little more than lip service to them for fifteen years. Working more collaboratively—and without all the baggage they'd been carrying around for so long—the team demonstrated incredible determination to work together to get things right. Everyone showed up early for the exercises and brought in innovative solutions and ideas. They were all fully engaged in the task at hand. The environment was respectful, productive, and energized. A number of exercises went so well that people broke into tears. They had come so far. They were on fire, and sustainable transformation was finally underway—and they could all feel the powerful shift. Everything about the leadership team changed for the positive and for good. They got it. The deep alignment and compelling future immersive workshops catapulted the company into the future. The company went on to get a $55 million strategic investment from a major tech giant and began thriving.

A stronger foundation led to a healthier culture, which changed everything for the better.

Liberating the Human Spirit

Here's the reality: just as you have liberated yourself through the work you've done as an individual, you must liberate the human spirit of each member of your executive team. People must move away from hopelessness, fear, and frustration toward courage, collaboration, engagement, and innovation. Ultimately, the goal is to reach a level of Synchronicity that leads to unprecedented effectiveness throughout the whole of the organization.

Change is simply not possible when people are mired in hopelessness, fear, and frustration. Like the team at Transtronic, your team can't move forward until you throw out the garbage and eliminate the VUCA. As a group, you must be willing to address and eliminate unhealthy entrenched behaviors and dynamics and make the necessary effort to build trust. Learn about one another and commit to a new, healthier way of thinking and behaving. If this work is done, the environment will shift from antagonistic and threatening to collaborative and respectful. There are no shortcuts. Once you begin to move people toward courage, engagement, innovation, and beyond, then—and only then—are you ready for a compelling future and building a framework for transformative, sustainable change within your organization.

KEY TAKEAWAYS

- Eighty percent of cultural transformations fail because the leadership team isn't willing to do the internal work necessary to make it real and sustainable—80 percent!

- Get your team into deep alignment with where you want to go, what you want to do, and what needs to change and improve to make it happen. Build trust.
- Invent new possibilities and a compelling future with your executive team to work together to create a noble cause and values for your organization, agree how decisions will be made through well-defined strategic anchors, align the leadership team around a thematic goal, and gain new perspectives on the power of accountability and integrity.
- Move beyond hopelessness, fear, and frustration to make room for courage, engagement, innovation, and synchronicity.

BRAINHACK

If you want to change the outputs your brain is producing, you have to change the inputs your brain is receiving. The thalamus acts as a gatekeeper in your brain. It takes in every input and decides what is important and what can be left behind. If every single input entered your brain, the electrical signals would be too much to handle, and you would pass out. The thalamus classifies each signal as one of three things: safe, not safe, or irrelevant. If your thalamus isn't functioning well, you might start to receive more information than is needed, or safe information might start to be labeled as unsafe. Your brain's default mode is protection, so the less energy it has, the more things it will label unsafe. Stimulating specific parts of the brain is like exercising a muscle—the more work it does, the stronger it will become. An easy way to exercise the thalamus is by closing your eyes and having someone tap your arm with one or two fingers. Your job is simply to determine how many fingers the person tapped you with. Doing so will upregulate your thalamus and strengthen the neural pathways in and around it.

POWERFUL QUESTIONS

- What is resonating for you in this chapter?
- What might be a Thematic Goal that could rally your team together and bring your business to the next level?
- What core values would support alignment with your thematic goal?
- How does your leadership team make decisions? Do you have a framework? If you implemented a decision-making framework, what do you anticipate as a challenge in operationalizing it?
- What is one thing you can commit to doing now?

CHAPTER 9

Trust is the Foundation of a High-Performance Culture

"Whoever is careless with truth in small matters cannot be trusted with important matters."

— ALBERT EINSTEIN —

The disintegration of trust is all around us—and not just at work. Trust in mainstream media hit an all-time low in 2021, according to data from Edelman's Trust Barometer. Trust in the US government also remains low, according to Pew research: "Since 2007, the share [of Americans] saying they can trust the government always or most of the time has not surpassed 30 percent." Even Gallup's polling data on the confidence level US adults have in their fellow Americans hit an all-time low in 2021. Business has not escaped this slide. Edelman's 2021 Trust Barometer discussed how the pandemic put "trust to the test" and recognized a crisis of leadership: "In particular CEOs' credibility is at all-time lows in several countries." Certainly, there is a correlation between these observations and the Great Resignation of 2021.

These are highly unsettling developments for anyone who leads people. You're trying to build trust in a world where trust has been broken across the board. This makes your work significantly more challenging. But in every crisis there is opportunity—and the current trust crisis is no exception. If you can build trust in your organization's culture, you have an opportunity to stand out in the crowd. And trust is worth the fight. Stephen Covey once said, "Trust is the glue of life. It's the most essential ingredient in effective communication. It's the foundational principle that holds all relationships." And this truth manifests in many benefits. Paul J. Zak, founding director of the Center for Neuroeconomics Studies and a professor of economics, psychology, and management at Claremont Graduate University, is one of many who have researched the topic. In a *Harvard Business Review* article called "The Neuroscience of Trust," he wrote:

> In my research I've found that building a culture of trust is what makes a meaningful difference. Employees in high-trust organizations are more productive, have more energy at work, collaborate better with their colleagues, and stay with their employers longer than people working at low-trust companies. They also suffer less chronic stress and are happier with their lives, and these factors fuel stronger performance.
>
> Leaders understand the stakes—at least in principle. In its 2016 *Global CEO Survey*, PwC reported that 55 percent of CEOs think that a lack of trust is a threat to their organization's growth. But most have done little to increase trust.

Zak's observation is especially disappointing in light of some of the other observations in the article:

> My team also found that those working in high-trust companies enjoyed their jobs 60 percent more, were 70 percent more aligned with their companies' purpose, and felt 66 percent closer to their colleagues. And a high-trust culture improves how people treat one another and themselves. Compared with employees at low-trust organizations, the high-trust folks had 11 percent more empathy for their workmates, depersonalized them 41 percent less often, and experienced 40 percent less burnout from their work. They felt a greater sense of accomplishment, as well—41 percent more.

Trust is clearly a gamechanger. So, why is there so little effort to build it within organizations? One reason is lack of know-how. It's a holistic problem that needs a holistic solution. It requires organizational-cultural expertise that most executive teams don't possess. Another reason trust building gets put on the back burner is that it's challenging and time consuming. Systemic distrust—which employees develop as a result of experiences with a company's rules, procedures, employees, and culture—plagues many companies. When consistency, accountability, and integrity are missing in these experiences, it's a breeding ground for systemic distrust, which negatively impacts performance and growth. Unfortunately, addressing systemic distrust with quick fixes like trust-building workshops or events won't get to the core of the problem, though this is the current toolkit used by many companies.

An intentional, multifaceted strategy is needed to build or rebuild systemic trust across an organization. As you're learning, trust building requires a strong foundation—a new level of self- and organizational awareness, openness, and commitment from an organization's leadership team. This type of important work takes time and focus—both rare commodities in today's harried, ever-changing business environment. It's easy for leadership teams to get stuck in the weeds, reacting to the crisis of the day and failing to make time for the type of transformational change that could shift the way they identify and tackle emerging issues *before* they become a crisis. I get it. As a leader, you have a lot on your plate. But here's the reality you face as you and your leadership team prepare to transform your organization's culture and break through to a new level of growth and innovation: trust is not optional. In order to speed up, your company must slow down. Make it a priority to do the individual and group work necessary to address the current VUCA and establish new behaviors and processes to build trust throughout your organization. It's worth the effort; you're creating the foundation for a sustainable, high-performance culture.

"Trust is fragile.
To build trust we must address distrust"
Fernando Flores

Trust Is Fragile

Warren Buffet once famously said, "It takes twenty years to build a reputation and five minutes to ruin it." It's true. Reputations are built on trust, and trust is fragile.

If you tell your employees and customers that one of your company values is integrity but don't walk the talk, trust is instantly broken. Words have little meaning if they aren't supported by actions and behaviors. If the executive team says integrity is important then engages in unethical activities, people will naturally say, "This company doesn't *really* value integrity." Actions speak louder than words. The words and actions of the leadership team matter a great deal. Leaders are held to very high standards, especially by employees. Remember the story I shared earlier about the 2015 Volkswagen scandal where the company deliberately falsified emissions tests? The company's stocks plummeted, it lost millions of dollars in revenue, and its reputation was badly damaged. What I didn't mention in that first telling was what happened with the company's employees. A July 2017 article in *Forbes*, "How Volkswagen Rallied Its Employees After Its Emissions Scandal (At Least for Now)," paints a grim picture. An employee at the Vienna-based employer-review platform called Kununu was interviewed about the dramatic shift in VW reviews after the scandal broke:

> The reviews show an unsurprisingly dramatic downturn in the wake of the ordeal, says Johannes Prüller, head of global communications for Kununu. "The company culture of Volkswagen was always about trust, integrity, reliability maybe," says Prüller. "With the scandal they somehow managed to put all of that at risk."

> "Before the scandal broke," Prüller explained, "if you compared the data we have for Volkswagen with BMW, Mercedes and also its own subsidiary, Audi, Volkswagen was rated best in almost every dimension of workplace satisfaction that we measure on Kununu." When news of its emissions testing misconduct emerged, those positive numbers tanked. "They were rated worst in twelve out of thirteen (dimensions)."

"To try to regain the favor of its demoralized staff," the article goes on to say, "VW employed a strategy of openness and outreach. 'They made sure that everyone knew what had happened and also what would happen next,' says Prüller. 'Just as they publicly admitted guilt in external communications . . . they had the same direct, face-to-face communication internally as well, as the first step in rebuilding trust.'"

Unfortunately, another VW scandal followed in the wake of the 2015 one, further damaging the company's reputation. For many, this was the straw that broke the camel's back. It would take many years for VW's culture to find its footing again. The disintegration of the human system's belief in their company's promises derailed all trust-building efforts. When trust is broken once, it takes time and effort to repair the damage. When trust is broken repeatedly, it can be challenging to reestablish. The lessons found in this chapter are straightforward: walk the talk and don't make promises you can't keep. These lessons seem simple, but for many companies they're not easy to execute. That's where the three Cs come in.

The Three Cs: Clear, Consistent Communication

Trust is the lynchpin of a healthy organizational culture. Without it, an executive team has nothing upon which to build meaningful, sustainable change. Where does trust live in an organization? In the conversations and behaviors that take place in the organization every day. To make sure trust is being built through these conversations and behaviors, you need the three Cs: clear, consistent communication. Without them, breakdowns occur easily.

When an executive team completes a deep alignment and compelling future program with my firm, they leave with a credo of their commitment to improve their organization and experience of working together for a common cause. They commit to building a more conscious and intentional organizational culture aligned with a freshly minted noble cause, mission, vision, and values. They commit to holding themselves accountable. They have moved from a state of hopelessness, fear, and frustration to a state of courage. Trust is the foundation of courage, and, like trust, courage is very fragile. In fact, courage is the most vulnerable and fragile state in any change effort. Just above the state of frustration that we discussed in the last chapter, courage is the first of the productive states. When people enter a state of courage, they *want* to believe. Their mindset has opened itself to the possibility that things could get better, and they're trying very hard to believe. But their belief is not yet solidified. Everyone is waiting to see if the new approach will stick or fall apart like other meaningless rah-rah management proclamations of the past. At any moment, something could undo the progress that has been made. It wouldn't take much for all the forward momentum to fall apart and regress. This is why courage and change are so fragile.

Done right, though, the three Cs can fortify trust and courage. Remember, trust is necessary for courage, and trust is built through clear, consistent communication, processes, and behavior. This is especially important in today's new normal. It keeps teams engaged, focused, and accountable. It is the vehicle that shapes work environments and drives positive behaviors, especially when leading distributed teams. Regardless of whether your team is in the office part time, full time, or still working from home, clear and frequent communication about the organization's status, priorities, customers, the marketplace, new initiatives, and progress toward existing initiatives helps employees understand what's happening. When people know what's going on, they don't have to count on back channeling and gossip for their information. But, when there's a lack of clear, authentic communication, employees are forced to fill in the blanks—which almost always leads to communication breakdowns. Conversely, in some companies, there is plenty of communication happening, but people are misinterpreting the message for a variety of reasons. Maybe they don't trust the message or the messenger because of previous communication issues. Maybe there are too many communication layers and some of the message is getting lost or changed along the way. Whatever the reason, this problem can also lead to communication breakdowns. If the leadership team wants to build trust, reinforce a new state of courage, align everyone around a noble cause, and drive sustainable change and high performance, an effective communications strategy is a must.

Commitment Counts

One of the most overlooked yet important challenges leaders encounter when trying to move a program, project, or initiative from idea to acceptance and implementation is commitment. In his profound collection of essays *Conversations for Action and Collected Essays*, Dr. Fernando Flores asks the question, "How do we produce results while at the same time developing relationships where we take care of each other in the process?" Flores answers by pointing to the importance of instilling a culture of commitment in working relationships, especially in our evolving work environments: "As teams become more virtual, distributed, and diverse, our ability to build trust, coordinate, and communicate with each other becomes both more essential and more difficult." He advocates for "pluralistic networks" in which people of different backgrounds, nationalities, cultures, and belief systems commit to working together, respecting one another's differences, and collaborating to create value for one another. It takes significant effort to navigate the inevitable challenges that will be encountered while trying to achieve this type of harmony. That's why Flores recommends work on what are often referred to as soft skills: the ability to cultivate trust and listen deeply as well as recognize, shift, and master our moods.

Unfortunately, organizations frequently underestimate the power of communication in general—much less the power of clear, consistent, authentic communication. Leaders assume their messages are being disseminated effectively when, in fact, they are not. Such assumptions mean communication breakdowns are often overlooked even as they wreak havoc on an organization's culture and performance. Companies that experience frequent communication breakdowns can get into big trouble—and fast. Forget about building courage and trust to ensure sustainable change; these companies are just trying to keep their heads above water. When we're called in to help, we typically find that there's no communication structure or strategy in place—or even awareness that one is needed. We start by bringing awareness to the domain of communication; we educate people on how people listen and what's in the way of listening fully. Through thoughtful conversation and discovery sessions, we help uncover barriers to effective communication for action.

We've seen many scenarios where CEOs have devoted significant time, energy, and money to orchestrate cultural change only to find a year or two later that no real progress has been made. The same problems are still happening, and the CEO's entire day is spent putting out fires. That's unhealthy and unsustainable. One of the first things we do when we're called in to help is conduct an ideal-versus-actual culture survey. The results show any number of issues, but they all share a common theme: a communication breakdown. After the survey results were reported to a recent client, the CEO was shocked to find that his leadership team was very resistant to the change but practiced cordial hypocrisy in order to keep the peace. In other words, they paid lip service to the change in meetings but didn't act on the initiatives in a meaningful way to actually bring about the change. This was revealed after nearly eighteen months of work with highly paid consultants who had plenty of ideas but didn't address the underlying communication issues that were sabotaging the entire effort. When time is so precious to busy CEOs, it's painful to watch this type of waste.

Learning to build a strong foundation for effective organizational communication as well as spot signs of breakdowns are both important skills that must be learned along the way. There are two sides to communications intelligence: one is understanding how people are listening; the other is understanding how speakers are communicating. We discussed this to a degree in earlier chapters, but it's worth examining it from a different angle. Communication is something the leadership team works on during our deep alignment and compelling future programs. But, when the leadership team rises to the fragile state of courage and prepares to bring a noble cause, mission, vision and values to the rest of the company, effective communication skills become absolutely central to success. The more people involved in a communication network—think human systems—the more important and challenging it becomes to have clear, consistent communication and behaviors.

When conversations take place between a speaker and a listener, the first thing that happens is the listener has a biochemical reaction to the speaker and what they're saying. If the reaction is positive, the listener is more open to hearing what they're saying and reacting in a conscious manner. However, if the communication is interpreted as negative or threatening in any way, the bioreaction hijacks the listener's attention—and often emotions. The listener is left with a skewed interpretation about what was said and why. In these cases, the speaker's message and intention can be lost. Growth and change can't happen without examining and improving communication.

Entire books have been written about communication and why and how people choose to be receptive to a message or not. The answers lie where communication and behavior meet. In other words, building trust through effective communication isn't just about the words we choose; it's about our relationship with the person to whom we're speaking. It's about our reputation and the type of rapport we have with others. It's about whether the message makes sense to the listener and whether the listener thinks the person speaking can be trusted, authentically cares about their needs, and has a believable message. It's about body language, tone, and the ability to "read" the listener's reaction. Magnify the complexity of individual conversations throughout an entire organization and you start to understand the intricacy of this dance for the CEO and leadership team. It takes skill and plenty of practice.

Training is a critical component to help leaders speak and listen more effectively. Everyone in a people-management role needs to learn these vital communication skills. Doing so will help them ask more questions and listen more openly for feedback. It will help them understand how their message is being interpreted by others. It will help them refine the delivery of their messages. When we work with companies that are stuck or struggling, we spend a lot of time training these crucial skills. Remember, in human systems, trust lives in our daily communications and behaviors. Whether the leadership team is getting communication wrong or right has a big impact on an organization's culture and performance. That's why our work with clients begins with situational and personal awareness and deep alignment, follows with developing a compelling future, and continues with communications intelligence. This gives aware and aligned leaders the opportunity to practice new levels and types of listening, interacting, and understanding. This type of training, when facilitated among a group of people who are committed, open, and willing, directly impacts the trust quotient between leaders, their followers, and the collective. Experiential programs offer plenty of opportunities to practice and engage. Mastery of these skills ensures the executive team gets communication right among themselves before taking their message of transformation to the company as a whole. This creates a strong foundation for cultural enrichment and the breakthrough performance that will follow.

Accountability

There's one last piece of the trust-building puzzle to discuss before the executive team can take its message of transformation to the organization level. It's necessary to fortify a state of courage and beyond. I'm talking about accountability. An environment of accountability—or lack thereof—starts with the CEO and leadership team. You can't hold others accountable if you're not holding yourself and your executive team accountable. Additionally, accountability must be baked into your communications strategy. Accountability doesn't exist without clear, consistent communication about the expectations and behaviors for which people will be held accountable. It simply wouldn't be fair. Unfortunately, this happens frequently for all the same reasons we explored in the last section. Many times, leaders don't even know there's a breakdown in communicating expectations and that it's disrupting an otherwise healthy environment of trust and accountability. For example, if the leadership team says it wants to build an environment of trust and accountability, but most mid-level managers are shaming and blaming their teams when goals aren't met, that's a big breakdown. I see these sorts of problems all the time. If you find this hard to believe, I invite you to reread the sections on self- and organizational awareness *and* blind spots. Then, ask the people you work with about their observations and assessments with regards to accountability in your organization. You might be surprised by what you find.

I have a great story to drive home these sorts of breakdowns. A couple of years ago, a midsize technology company sent one of their talented up-and-coming female leaders to one of our Ignite Your Power trainings. These events are designed specifically for emerging leaders. Before the event, company leaders warned us that this young woman—we'll call her Sarah—was very talented but would be skeptical of our methods, have trouble participating in key activities, and be closed minded. When we met Sarah, we had the opposite experience. She was open to every lesson and opportunity we offered. She participated fully. At the end of the three-day event, she stood before a room full of our trainers and fellow emerging female leaders and shared openly and gratefully how much she had learned.

"Thank you," she said. "This training has been excellent. I am energized, awakened, and enriched as a leader. I can't wait to take everything I've learned back to my company. I just wonder why they only sent me when it's obvious that the current leadership team also needs to do this training as soon as possible" Everyone laughed, but Sarah had hit the nail on the head: The current leadership team thought the problem was Sarah, but it wasn't. *It was all of them!* Sarah trusted us and the safe environment we had created for her and others at the Ignite Your Power event. As a result, she was able to bring her authentic, highest self to the exercises and training we offered. Sarah didn't trust the executive team at her company, so she was naturally skeptical and hesitant about the things they said and asked of her. The leadership team at her organization was asking emerging leaders to do work that they weren't willing to do themselves. Think about the message this sends to the organization as a whole. It was time for the leadership team to become more accountable for its behaviors and the impact of those behaviors on the mood and behaviors of their human system. There couldn't be a foundation for transformation until they did the work that they were asking others to do.

Clear, consistent communication topped off with a serving of accountability is the breakfast of champions. When people know how effective communications are conducted things run smoothly. When everyone understands the rewards and consequences for certain behaviors, more positive behaviors are shaped. This creates an environment conducive to transformation. When agreements are simple, straightforward, and consistently honored, trust is built, courage is fortified, and the organization's culture is primed for breakthrough growth. This is the power of trust, the three Cs, and accountability when it comes to shaping high-performance organizational cultures.

KEY TAKEAWAYS

- Trust is foundational for sustainable growth and change, yet it is very fragile.
- Trust lives in conversations. Practice clear, consistent communication.
- When trust is broken, it can and should be repaired and restored, and the only way to do this is through open and honest communication.

- There are two sides to communications intelligence: one concerns understanding and adjusting how people are listening, the other understanding and adjusting how speakers are communicating.

BRAINHACK

Our brains function by predicting patterns about the world. When something is reliable, it is less stressful because the patterns we predict are usually correct. But, when something is unreliable, our brains produce a threat response, as the patterns it keeps predicting are wrong. This is why trust is so important at work. If the workplace is reliable and people trust one another, the brain's patterns of prediction will produce a "safe" response, and work will be significantly less stressful. If, however, there is no trust in the workplace, the brain's patterns will produce a "threat" signal, and work will be associated with stress and fear. If you find yourself in an untrusting environment, practice small things every day to ease the patterns your brain predicts. Try to have a set routine for the workday, take regularly scheduled breaks, and map out your tasks at the beginning and end of each day. Ease the strain on your brain and give it some safe patterns. You can't always control your environment, but you can do things to make that environment more manageable.

POWERFUL QUESTIONS

- What is resonating for you in this chapter?
- How do you hold yourself accountable for your own clear communication with your team and your company?
- What happens to you, or anyone at your company, when accountability fails?

CHAPTER 10

A Structure for Dismantling Roadblocks

"Only those who dare to fail greatly can ever achieve greatly."

—ROBERT F. KENNEDY—

A n organization's transformation journey rarely looks like a hockey stick of change and growth in the beginning. That happens later. A steep, winding mountain road is a more accurate description of the first part of the trek. Roadblocks, setbacks, and surprises are around every corner. But, after the individual and group work you've done, you're fit for the climb. And the destination is definitely worth it. When the spirit of the human system is ignited at work, everyone can see the future together, and it is theirs. Now clearly distinguished from the competition, this peak-performance human organization can look out at the valley below—strewn with companies paralyzed by fear, dysfunction, and underperformance—and shout from the mountaintops, "Not us!" Organizations willing to do transformative work always win. This has been proven in case study after case study. There's no disputing the benefits of the rigorous journey ahead. I believe you and your leadership team will find the courage to fully commit—hopefully, you've already found it.

Knowing the journey will be long, it's worth setting up a framework to distribute the weight you have to carry up the mountain, prevent roadblocks en route, and dismantle them when they inevitably occur. Your organization's human system must be prepared to learn by failing forward until reaching the summit. The framework we recommend is based on Liberating Structures, which are designed to upend the old and increasingly ineffective top-down, command-and-control leadership style found in many of today's corporate cultures. As co-creators of the Liberating Structures concept, Keith McCandless and Henri Lipmanowicz explain:

> Liberating Structures productively disrupt conventional patterns in how we work together. They change dramatically the way results are generated without expensive investments, complicated training, or dramatic shifts in organizational structures. . . . Liberating Structures introduce tiny shifts in the way we meet, plan, decide, and relate to one another. They put the innovative power once reserved for experts only in the hands of everyone. [They are] a set of simple microstructures from which individuals and groups can choose what suits their likes and dislikes then mix and match them flexibly to address their challenges.

By focusing first on the structures to support a company's human system—rather than the behavior and performance of the people in that system—the executive team creates a strong foundation for sustainable change and growth—and *this* is what makes all the difference in the journey. In an environment of trust and accountability, Liberating Structures support agile human systems in which people are capable of assessing problems and finding effective solutions quickly. This builds trust and leads to alignment and deeper interconnectedness within the whole of the human system. As

McCandless and Lipmanowicz have found in their work, Liberating Structures "reveal an immense source of untapped knowledge, capability, and momentum."

McCandless and Lipmanowicz have created more than thirty microstructures to facilitate communication and problem solving. From "Improv Prototyping" to "Wicked Questions" to "Appreciative Interviews," each microstructure has a different approach, feel, and function, giving people a wide selection of structures to meet their specific needs and styles. For example, "Wise Crowds" make it possible for individuals to tap into the wisdom of a whole group in rapid fifteen-minute cycles. As McCandless and Lipmanowicz explain:

> **Wise Crowds** make it possible to instantly engage a small or large group of people in helping one another. You can set up a **Wise Crowds** consultation with one small group of four or five people or with many small groups simultaneously or, during a larger gathering, with a group as big as one hundred or more people. Individuals, referred to as "clients," can ask for help and get it in a short time from all the other group members. Each individual consultation taps the expertise and inventiveness of everyone in the group simultaneously. Individuals gain more clarity and increase their capacity for self-correction and self-understanding. **Wise Crowds** develop people's ability to ask for help. They deepen inquiry and consulting skills. Supportive relationships form very quickly. During a **Wise Crowds** session, the series of individual consultations makes the learning cumulative as each participant benefits not only from being a client but also from being a consultant several times in a row. **Wise Crowds** consultations make it easy to achieve transparency. Together, a group can outperform the expert!

With more than thirty Liberating Structures to choose from, any individual or team can find the right microstructure to fit their needs, build trust among the troops, and tap into the collective intelligence of the team. In my organization, we facilitate Liberating Structures in all of our executive sessions, retreats, and immersion workshops. We have even found ways to integrate Liberating Structures into our remote and online training courses.

Liberate Through Language

Through individual and group effort, training, practice, and discipline, you and your leadership team have prepared yourselves for transformation. You're almost ready to take what you've learned to the rest of your organization's human system. You're ready to walk the talk and deliver on your promises. People won't just hear a message from on high this time; they'll *experience* the changes as you and your leadership team demonstrate a new mindset and set of positive behaviors that support and inspiring noble cause, mission, vision and values. And you'll have Liberating Structures in place for problem solving, innovation, feedback, and refinement.

At this critical juncture, your highest self must fully tune in to the individuals in your organization's human system. This means people within the organization not only understand Zaffron and Logan's three laws of performance, covered earlier, but that they are learning to work with one another according to these laws. As discussed, perspective and language are both intrinsic to communication. Leaders who understand this can spot the root cause of most communication breakdowns. By addressing the root cause of a problem, leaders can create more sustainable solutions to repair breakdowns—or even prevent them altogether.

We all have different DNA and life experiences, and they shape how we see the world. We create our own realities. That's why *our perceptions shape our performance.* Even when we're all working on the same problem with the same facts, the problem *occurs* to us differently. This is a key insight into human behavior. Leaders who recognize that their reality might not be the same as someone else's have a distinct advantage over those who rely on the more traditional "my way or the highway" point of view. Imagine walking into a meeting with more self- and organizational awareness as well as empathy. How would that change your interactions with the individuals in the room? Dramatically, right? This is one reason why Liberating Structures are so important and work so well. They distribute the discovery process so that everyone in the organization's human system is communicating and problem solving with the first law in mind. Once individuals in small groups sort through the hodgepodge of perspectives on any given subject, the best ideas can bubble up. This means less resistance and more momentum.

Liberating structures are built and sustained through language, which has a profound impact on our thoughts, feelings, moods, and behaviors. As we've explored in previous chapters, roadblocks happen *inside* communication. The words we use and how we communicate influences how our message is received by others. Body language and tone of voice also matter. Language shapes how we experience the world today and in the future. Most of us have ingrained patterns of communication that we unknowingly repeat—and some are negative. These negative communication patterns can hinder effective communications and damage relationships. Overcoming these old patterns takes training, practice, and patience. Because these skills are so important for leadership teams—especially as they navigate the early, precarious days of transformative change—it's something we tackle in our deep alignment and compelling future immersion workshops with executive teams. We encourage all the leaders we work with to master all skills that lead to effective communication. Keep honing your own communication skills and watch how it shifts your thoughts, feelings, moods, and behaviors. Then, bring what you've learned to your executive team and beyond to show how new, more productive communication patterns will help them replace unproductive thoughts, feelings, moods, and behaviors. Over time, this will have a profound and positive ripple effect throughout the organization.

Our brain's default wiring lets past experiences define our future. This can be altered with practice, but most people don't even have the self-awareness to recognize this limiting thinking and behavior, much less change it. "Last year's numbers indicate we're on track for 3 percent growth." "We never win those larger contracts. Let's keep targeting the midsize ones." These statements use descriptive language. If you take a closer look at both statements, you'll see clearly that each describes the future with language about the past. There's nothing inspiring in either of those statements. If you want to transform how things occur to people, you have to help them shift their perspective by using future-based language.

Remember the story about President John F. Kennedy's vision to put a human on the moon by 1969? When Kennedy spoke about this, do you think he used descriptive language? Indeed, he did not. Do you think he could have rallied the nation, even the world, around his ideas by saying, "We have never put a human on the moon before, but we hope to do so soon"? That's not an inspiring message and would have been unlikely to shift people's perspectives. In order to help others see what he could see—without much evidence, I might add—Kennedy used future-based language—called generative language. If you want to see this type of language in action, watch JFK's 1962 speech at Rice University, "Why Go to the Moon?" He begins by reframing how we think about the timeline of history. He addresses the descriptive framing of the idea by naysayers head on to shift their perspective and reorient it toward a more promising future:

> It is not surprising that some would have us stay where we are a little longer to rest, to wait. But this city of Houston, this State of Texas, this country of the United States was not built by those who

waited and rested and wished to look behind them. This country was conquered by those who moved forward—and so will space.

William Bradford, speaking in 1630 of the founding of the Plymouth Bay Colony, said that all great and honorable actions are accompanied with great difficulties, and both must be enterprised and overcome with answerable courage.

If this capsule history of our progress teaches us anything, it is that man, in his quest for knowledge and progress, is determined and cannot be deterred. The exploration of space will go ahead, whether we join in it or not, and it is one of the great adventures of all time, and no nation which expects to be the leader of other nations can expect to stay behind in the race for space.

Those who came before us made certain that this country rode the first waves of the industrial revolutions, the first waves of modern invention, and the first wave of nuclear power, and this generation does not intend to founder in the backwash of the coming age of space. We mean to be a part of it. We mean to lead it. For the eyes of the world now look into space, to the moon and to the planets beyond, and we have vowed that we shall not see it governed by a hostile flag of conquest, but by a banner of freedom and peace. We have vowed that we shall not see space filled with weapons of mass destruction, but with instruments of knowledge and understanding.

Yet the vows of this Nation can only be fulfilled if
we in this nation are first, and, therefore, we intend
to be first.

Now, *that* is generative language in action! Kennedy's speeches
transfixed the world and reshaped its perspective on what was possible. He told the world what was going to happen next, and then
he made it happen. As you and your executive team lead your company into the next phase of growth, you must always be listening
for the future and reshaping the language used to describe it. It's
time to shake old, unproductive communication patterns and use
future-based language to communicate the transformation you want
to see. Self-awareness, training, and practice will make perfect.

FIXED(STUCK)

- Command and Control
- My Way or the Highway
- Profit driven
- Hierarchy, fiefdom
- Money is main barometer of success
- Silos, Turf Wars, Infighting
- Frustration & Fear are ever present
- Fixed mindset
- VUCA
- Adrenaline Bias
- Task Driven
- People bring routine to work

EMERGENT

- Noble Cause driven
- Shared leadership
- Courage, Engagement and Innovation are ever present
- Self Managing Teams
- Expansive energy
- Possibility is ever present
- Stakeholder value is the barometer of success
- People centric
- Growth Mindset
- Congruent Values
- Unrivaled Innovation
- Instrictic motivation
- People bring genius to work

Emergent Cultures

When an organization's human system has trust, alignment, accountability, and the interconnectivity and momentum created by Liberating Structures and effective communication, it becomes unstoppable. Everyone starts to move in sync. If you've ever seen birds flocking or fish schooling, you've seen what is called "emergent behavior." Despite having no leader or central control, these creatures move together in perfect synchronicity. They do amazing things, and it looks effortless. Emergent behaviors are made possible by high levels of interconnectivity.

Igniting the human spirit at work unleashes massive interconnectivity. And, when you allow this to happen in an environment of trust—where individuals are aligned around a noble cause, values they believe in, and a strong vision for the future—you've created an environment conducive to an emergent culture. As the leadership team prepares to shift from transforming itself to inspiring and transforming an entire human system, an emergent culture should be their guiding light. This type of culture is built on a framework that enables continuous assessment; powerful and effective communication; healthy, ongoing growth and positive change; human alignment; and high performance. Breakthroughs are common at companies with emergent cultures because leadership isn't defined as overseeing people or giving orders from the C-suite. At top-performing companies, the leadership team's mandate is to create an environment for ongoing evolution and transformation. Leaders build cultures where the people in the organization's human system can operate at their highest level, both individually and collectively. Synchronicity, innovation, extreme ownership, momentum, and high performance are the norm within emergent cultures.

KEY TAKEAWAYS

- Set up a framework to distribute responsibilities, prevent roadblocks, and dismantle them when they inevitably occur. Your organization's human system must be prepared to learn by failing forward.
- Realize that none of us sees things as they are. We see how things occur to us. Master generative, future-based language.
- Hone your own communication skills, and help others improve theirs. Then, watch how it positively impacts everyone's thoughts, feelings, moods, and behaviors.

BRAINHACK

The best way to overcome a bad habit is to create a new one and repeat that new habit over and over and over again. If you find that you're bad at communicating, the only way to get better is to practice clear and intentional communication repeatedly. Repetition strengthens the neural pathways in the brain that correlate with that habit. The more you do a bad habit, the more challenging it will be to break it. But if you create a good habit for yourself and constantly repeat it, you are less likely to slide back into that bad habit. So, make a goal for yourself with communication. Commit to something small and manageable. For example, the next time you have a conversation for action, start the conversation with your why, follow it up with the problem your request will solve, and complete the communication with the definition of successful completion and the date by when you need the request complete. Once your conversation is complete in your mind, ask the receiver of the project, task, or request to reiterate their understanding. This slowing-down process will help you be understood and will create powerful conversations for action that give the receiver a complete understanding of the request. Continue to make requests with this four-step process as it turns it into a healthy habit. Repetition is key to creating healthy habits.

POWERFUL QUESTIONS

- What is resonating for you in this chapter?
- What are some ideas you have for improvements in how your human system works together, builds trust, and coordinates actions to fulfill your noble cause?
- What will be needed from you as the leader? What strengths can you draw on?
- Emergent behaviors and liberating structures are catalyst to achieve the culture you yearn for. What inspiring actions can you take now?

If you want to take your learning journey to the next level, I have created a series of trainings that support you in, deepening your learning while equipping you in getting into action to cultivate the kind of culture required to be a market leader.

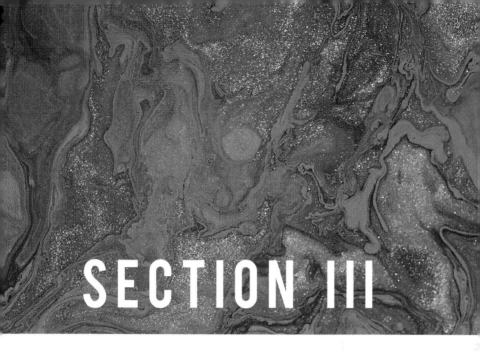

SECTION III

The Organization

Is It Ready for Breakthrough Performance?

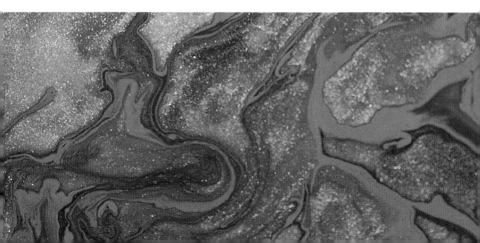

CHAPTER 11

The Alchemy of Enduring High Performance

"Victories aren't born on the field. You create them during practice—day in and day out."

— SILVIA PENCAK —

C hange is a never-ending journey. Everyone needs to keep growing—you, your executive team, and your people. But stop here if any of you are still struggling with the basics. You can't skip ahead in this process. If you as a CEO or your executive team are still exhibiting dysfunctional behaviors, then the company is still dysfunctional. Hopefully, having read *Ignite Culture* this far, you have course corrected and built a strong foundation of self- and organizational awareness to bring transformation to your entire organization. Dysfunction has a powerfully negative trickle-down effect. If you don't fix the dysfunction at the top, you can never achieve positive, lasting change within the whole of the organization's human system.

Moving ideas from a small group to a large one is a delicate dance where trust is essential. All your efforts could fall apart during this vulnerable transition if the people impacted by the changes don't believe that the organization's leadership will stand by the changes in the face of resistance, complacency, or other inevitable challenges. The human system must believe that sustainable change is possible. Engage the hearts and minds of your people. It's essential, though it's no small task. This is why a solid foundation must be in place before moving forward.

If you and your team are ready, this section is all about the psychology of change and achievement. What does it mean for your organization to be an intentional, healthy, high-performing emergent culture? What does that look like? What does is *not* look like? How do you help employees find and experience self-actualization through their work and learn the power of achieving more together in alignment and with your company's core values and in service of its noble cause? Don't let the adrenaline bias hijack this fragile phase of change. A holistic, mindful plan is required, a plan that considers the practical and human psychology of change. There's no quick fix when it comes to culture. It takes time to develop the framework (systems, processes, infrastructure) and environment conducive to lasting change. I know you're busy and probably juggling too much. I understand. You just want to get it done. But now is the time to slow down and focus on the most important thing—igniting the full potential of the organization's human system. When a culture aligns around core values and a noble purpose, it becomes emergent, and everything speeds up dramatically. Friction and VUCA are replaced with interconnectedness, trust, and alignment. *This* is how you win your market with the full support of a healthy, high-performance team. Change initiatives fail all too often because leadership teams don't give the change initiative the bandwidth, focus, and time it needs. Take the necessary time to orchestrate intentional, transformative, and lasting change. This is the essence of your job as a leader. There can be no higher priority.

High-Performance Alchemy

Alchemy is the process of taking something ordinary and turning it into something extraordinary, sometimes in ways that can't be explained. When people are inspired, progressing, growing, innovating, creating, and maintaining transformation together, amazing things start to happen. An emergent, evolutionary human system has been created. By definition, this type of system is built to continue growing, improving, and responding positively to the inevitable challenges ahead. Emergent, evolutionary human systems are characterized by unrivaled innovation, intrinsic motivation, and exceptional teamwork. Left behind is the entangled culture that once held your company back. Ignited is exponential growth that is fueled by the organization's inspired and empowered human potential. Everyone wants and expects big things to happen. You've successfully ignited the human spirit at work. An environment exist where people can operate as their highest and best self every day. Their life purpose and personal goals can be achieved *because* they work with your organization, not in spite of that fact. Everyone is aligned around what needs to be achieved, and they're accountable for making it happen.

In this type of healthy, humanistic, and high-growth environment, no one needs to be pushed and prodded to perform; no one needs to be forced to take responsibility. Everyone is achievement oriented. They are self-motivated and working toward common goals. They clearly understand their role in achieving those goals and accept full ownership of that role. There are no more command and control statements from on high—no more "It's my way or the highway!" There's also no micromanagement in a self-actualized culture. The environment is free of competitive or oppositional behavior. Negative behaviors squash self-actualization, so they aren't tolerated. In healthy, humanistic, emergent cultures, people get the opportunity and autonomy to work and live as their highest, best selves. They are in charge of their own destiny. People are self-actualizing together. People are fully contributing because they believe they can influence the future and help make the organization's noble cause a reality. The workday is affiliative. People feel connected and are working collaboratively because they believe they can achieve more together than alone. They feel valued and respected by the company's leadership and their colleagues. Rather than being sand in the gears, every individual is working to embody the organization's values and achieve its mission. They work through problems and fix what's not working. No one is paralyzed by fear, the possibility of failure, or the thought of being pulled into a yelling match. Those days are gone—and, if you do this right, they'll never come back. If and when trouble starts brewing, you and your people will be able to spot the signs, diagnose the real issue, and address the problem with effective communication and trust. In turn, the team interdependently redirects efforts through utilizing the Liberating Structures and recalibrates to solve their problems together.

We've already talked about Microsoft as a model for this type of organizational transformation. But, in their book *Incremental to Exponential*, authors Vivek Wadhwa and Ismail Amla document the magnitude of the transition at Microsoft as well as the astounding results of its cultural shift:

> When Satya Nadella was named the CEO of Microsoft, in February 2014, one of his first acts was to ask all the top executives at the famously combative software company to read Marshall Rosenberg's *Nonviolent Communication*, a book about how to communicate and collaborate effectively using compassion and understanding rather than competition and judgment.
>
> With that request, Nadella signaled to the company's leaders that he wanted to make a big change in the culture of the world's largest software company.

Bill Gates, the company's longtime CEO, had been known for berating employees. Steve Ballmer, who succeeded Gates, made cringe-worthy YouTube bait with his on-stage screaming and sweaty-faced antics at company product launches. Both endorsed hard-ball business tactics that competitors feared and admired but customers and most employees loathed.

Nadella was cut from a different cloth. Calm, and described by some as beatific, Nadella was born in India and has an enduring love of cricket. He also embraces Buddhist beliefs and has long enjoyed a reputation for calm responses even in the most contentious circumstances and for focusing on positive feedback to reinforce good habits.

As a manager and a leader, too, Nadella made it clear that the old, aggressive behaviors were no longer welcome. Never raising his voice or showing overt anger at employees or executives, Nadella constantly worked to create a more comfortable environment. He never wrote angry emails, and he refused to tolerate anger or yelling in executive meetings.

At the same time, he promoted a culture of curiosity and learning. He urged the company's 120,000+ employees to embrace a "learn-it-all" curiosity, in contrast to what he categorized as Microsoft's traditional "know-it-all" worldview. In the marathon Friday executive-team meetings, Nadella instituted a regular feature wherein Microsoft researchers would phone in to talk about their innovations— reminding the company's leaders of the company's advances and encouraging them to focus on the future rather than maintain the status quo. . . . The results of Nadella's efforts have been nothing short of spectacular. The company's market capitalization has nearly increased by an order of magnitude, from roughly $300 billion at Nadella's ascension to about $2.5 trillion today, and Microsoft has become the most valuable company in the world, surpassing Apple and Google.

Microsoft's transformation provides a tangible example of how the alchemy of healthy high performance manifests in a human system. It requires clear values, a noble cause, and a group discipline modeled from the top. Let's explore the organizational mindset shift that is necessary to orchestrate the type of significant, intentional, and sustainable cultural change seen at Microsoft.

Elevating Performance

As your organization enters this new and still fragile phase of cultural transformation, everyone is excited about a new way of being and doing at work. However, they're still afraid. They worry that the change won't stick. They want to believe, but they've been inspired before only to have their hopes dashed. They've put in the effort before only to see things go south again after a few months. Those leaders who strive for true organizational change must be cognizant of these fears and understand their roots. Toxic past behaviors by management and colleagues will linger in people's minds until new, positive behaviors arise and are perceived to be permanent. Creating a new normal takes time, discipline, and effort. You and your team of change agents must be prepared to navigate a long transition period filled with booby traps.

In the beginning of any change initiative, the past is ever present. Most people have ideas about the future that are shaped by old self-limiting beliefs and often negative past experiences. You and your leadership team are there to help them envision a better future—like the one you've created for yourselves. It can be challenging to achieve hope and optimism at scale. Knowing Zaffron and Logan's three laws of performance and abiding by them are two separate activities. The latter requires the adoption of a number of important new behavioral disciplines. These disciplines help people and organizations adopt a more hopeful narrative around change, which is key.

The 3 Dimensions of Cultural Evolution
From Entangled Culture to Emergent Culture

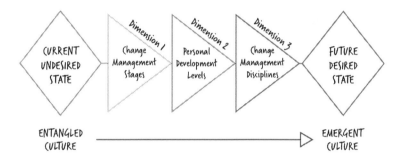

Disciplines of Change

Many leaders rise to the top of organizations because of their achievements, not because they have advanced organizational psychology degrees. This is why it's worth exploring foundational truths about human performance and discipline in more depth. Now that you've enrolled the collective in the possibility of a new future, you're ready to inspire change through collective action. There are actually seven disciplines that must be developed to create transformational change. Each is valuable on its own, but, collectively, they add up to more than the sum of their parts. When these disciplines are practiced in an organization, the ground is fertile for people within the organization to experience self-actualization in their role through service to the noble cause, which, in turn, creates fertile ground for emergent behavior—the secret sauce of sustainable high performance. Emergent behavior occurs when an entity is observed to have properties or behaviors that only emerge when the parts interact seamlessly as a wider whole. For example, a lone fish can try to outswim a predator. It can zig and zag and swim up or down, but the fish's odds of survival are not so good alone. A school of fish, on the other hand, can move in synchronicity with simple behaviors to confuse a predator, increasing their odds of survival significantly. You might have seen this type of swarm-like behavior during a nature program or in the wild. Earlier, we mentioned this behavior with swarming birds. Emergent behaviors and their benefits aren't something an individual can achieve. But, as a group working together, emergent behaviors offer many benefits. For humans, they actually enable self-actualization *together*. When leaders start to see and experience emergent behaviors throughout their organization's human system, they have achieved cultural transformation. The human spirit has truly been unleashed at work. The effort of each individual remains valuable on its own, but the energy released by the human system working together toward a common goal has an exponential effect.

A couple of years ago, we worked with a highly successful CEO in Silicon Valley. The company she led had grown exponentially. They knew their customers, and their sales team hit it out of the ballpark. They did great work but had never slowed down to create a foundation and architecture to support their growth. There was no noble cause or any company values. There was no commitment or structure in place to ensure effective communication, ownership, or accountability as the organization's head count grew. As they hit a growth inflection point, things started to unravel. They threw money at the problem and hired several consultants to address specific issues. But they didn't step back to look at their problems holistically. They started to lose their customers' trust. Their employees became more and more polarized as everyone played the blame game. The CEO didn't understand why her efforts to fix the problems and make changes weren't working. She met one on one with employees. No one was giving her any solutions. They were just complaining.

She and her leadership team flew in for a deep alignment, and we studied the results of the organization's ideal-versus-actual culture survey. There was a lot of mistrust and frustration with broken agreements. She and her leadership team seemed perplexed. They felt they were good at keeping their agreements. Next, everyone agreed to behavioral ground rules for our sessions—one was being on time for meetings. After a break, three people walked in ten minutes late. They were oblivious to the fact that they had already broken one of the agreements they had made just an hour earlier. At first, people were hesitant to call out this behavior. Then, one person spoke up.

"We never keep our agreements."

Another added, "I've waited for key people to arrive for meetings for more than an hour. It's not uncommon."

Now people were getting braver. "It's true, and one-on-one meetings are promised but then constantly rescheduled."

The only people in the discussion who didn't contribute to the conversation were the three people who had arrived late after the break. I asked them why they decided it was okay to be late.

"I had to call my nanny," the first person shared.

The second admitted, "I just didn't take the agreement that seriously."

And the third person said, "There was a line for the bathroom."

We discussed how widespread the distrust was within their organization and the fact that the distrust grew because of so many broken agreements over little and big things. They got it, they felt it, and they committed to change. Within six months, their net promoter with customers had gone up by 1.5 percent. The CEO started calling customers to find out what had changed. Over and over, she heard that the tone and commitment of the company's front-line employees had improved—all because they were keeping their commitments and agreements.

Messages of trust can be shared in meetings and company communications ad nauseum but are meaningless if not anchored in a noble cause and a strong set of values that are practiced and honed every day. Change is built on trust, and trust is built in the small, daily moments that everyone experiences in the halls of your organization. If people aren't walking the talk, sustainable and meaningful change isn't possible.

As authors Solomon and Flores say in *Building Trust*, "Building trust begins with an honest understanding of trust, but it also requires everyday routines and practices. Without the practices, that understanding comes to nothing." Shifting routines and behaviors takes discipline. So, which disciplines must be practiced to support transformative change in a human system? All people in the system must practice:

- **Conscious use of self.** In order to be part of effective change in a human system, people have to become more self-aware and intentionally bring their whole being and best use of self to the change movement. This means understanding, being aware of, and catching habituated responses and reactions that hinder progress—and cleaning up the impact of unhealthy reactions when they occur. Individuals must learn to tune in to their innate intelligence, turn on their creative genius, and take action in their unique role so that innovation and synchronicity can be achieved by the whole.

- **Whole-systems orientation.** This means individuals think as much about the big picture as themselves. They understand how their actions, potential decisions, and changes to a process may impact stakeholders in the whole. They respect that a framework is required to aid people in working together to create and support change. This is what emergence is all about.

- **Openness to sound and current data.** Organizations need sound and current data to make informed decisions. Since we know that perception of facts matters more than the facts themselves, it's important that everyone in the organization at every level accepts that data can help them more clearly see reality rather than their perception of it. While the reality may not always be pretty, leaders must utilize data's power to identify issues and systemic breakdowns, make critical business decisions, and take action when and where needed.
- **Constructive feedback.** This is an essential component in a healthy, intentional, and high-performance culture because it gives both the sender and the receiver the opportunity to partner and grow in service of the noble cause. On an individual level, it also develops competency in communication. Communication isn't only about compliments, accolades, rainbows, and butterflies. There are times, especially during change, that discussions must focus on what needs to be different or improved. This includes redirection and correction. All employees at every level in a constructive culture learn to speak and listen from a place of possibility versus a place of defense. The speaker learns to analyze the effect of his or her message and ensure that the receiver has interpreted the message correctly. Since the three laws of performance make it clear that one person's perception of reality is not another's, constructive feedback provides a crucial process for clarification, understanding, and message refinement. Sustainable change can't happen without it.
- **Respect for the collective intelligence.** When individuals realize that they don't always have to be right in order to produce results, everything shifts. In an emergent culture, collective intelligence is always greater than the sum of its individual brainpower. This thinking improves the quality of relationships within the human system because it's affiliative and collaborative. Conflict management is replaced

by open communication and constructive problem solving. Liberating Structures that enable individuals to get out of their own way, stop themselves and the team from looking backwards, and move into inclusive, generative problem solving allow the team to operate fluidly and innovate.

- **Learning from differences.** As Einstein famously said, "We can't solve problems by using the same kind of thinking we used when we created them." Organizations need to tap into the unique genius of their people and teams to get the kind of new thinking required to change, grow, and innovate. When organizations create an inclusive and safe space for the open exchange of ideas between people with diverse backgrounds, experiences, and ideas, they have a much better chance of creating lasting and transformational change.

- **Empowerment.** When leaders empower their people to navigate change using Liberating Structures, they create space for the human system's collective intelligence. The change actually sticks when the people affected are fully empowered to solve problems and confront challenges together. Liberating Structures provide the necessary framework for individuals and teams in the human system to make effective decisions about how to shape their collective future. When people are aligned around the company's values, vision, mission, and noble cause and empowered to drive growth, innovation, and continuous improvement through Liberating Structures, they choose solutions in step with the vision of the whole. This instills emergent behaviors, which always empower both the individual and the whole.

The Process of Transformation

A typical culture transformation takes between eighteen to thirty-six months, depending on the size of the company. For larger organizations, it might take five years. Michael F. Broom is an organizational psychologist, author, executive coach, and organizational facilitator with more than thirty years of experience. He's also the CEO and president of the Center for Human Systems. In my opinion, his five-step meta model for planned change is the best guide through this pivotal, precarious phase in your organization's transformation. We use Broom's process in our organizational training and consulting. Here are Broom's five steps:

> **Contracting**—This is the process of coming to agreement with other key stakeholders in the success of a change project. When organizational change is the goal, this contracting must be made between the highest level of management in the organization. Effective transformation agreements and conversations for action need to specify clear goals that are internally consistent and aligned with the organization's noble cause and values. Roles must be clearly defined for everyone signing the contract. Once there is agreement on the direction, objectives, and goals, then leadership can move the initiative forward to the collective. This ensures an effective, collaborative, inclusive, and empowering change process.

> **Data Gathering**—Once the initial contract has been established, the change-effort team should start gathering data to inform their efforts as well as alert and excite the organization about the coming change. They'll want to find out what's working, what needs improvement, what is currently being done, what are the roadblocks, and what is the current thinking about the change efforts.

Intervening—All change requires effective human relationships, so putting in place an architecture to improve relationships is important. Interventions include such activities as creating a feedback system, team-building events, immersion workshops, ongoing coaching, conflict management, and so on. You either need someone internally who's an extraordinary group facilitator and conflict manager, or you need to bring someone in with these skills. Intervening requires courage, deep listening, neutrality, and straight talk as well as an understanding of the whole system.

Evaluating—Change is an iterative process. It's a journey. You must have regular check-in points—think agile methodology. This means different levels of evaluation are happening daily, weekly, and monthly—not just annually. No more one-time workshops. This is a whole new way of being. The change team must always be gathering feedback and evaluating it for continued improvement. Sometimes, periodic evaluations mean asking an individual about how they feel the change effort is going, while other times it is a company-wide questionnaire. What's important is that an ongoing feedback process is in place so people feel heard and so the change team can see what's working and what's not.

Disengagement—Even though change and growth will be ongoing within the organization, there should be a distinguishable end to the first major transformation project. You might have a closing evaluation session, create a statement of what has been learned, or throw a party to celebrate the achievement of this milestone and acknowledge people's contributions. Whatever it is, it should create a sense of closure and allow the change agents to move on effectively to what's next.

Remember 80% of organizational change efforts fail because no structure existed to support and sustain the change. Don't make this mistake. Create a sustainable framework for success before you go wide with your ideas—and make sure the right people, your key agents of change, are fully on board and understand the goals and their role in achieving transformational change. Effective organization and communication are key. The baton must be passed from the initial catalysts for change to those people now living with its implementation. New roles and responsibilities need to be designed around the transformation for the long-term health and welfare of your ever-changing and growing human system. In an organization embarking on a cultural journey, the CEO is always devoting at least a quarter of his or her time specifically to understanding, intervening, and inspiring their organization's culture. For larger organizations, there needs to be a support team created to partner with the CEO. However, it's important to remember that ownership for an organization's culture can never fully be delegated. An inspired culture must remain core to everything the CEO and executive team do. It must be part of the continuum.

The Culture Kickoff

I believe a culture kickoff is an important ritual to mark the moment in an organization's history when a new future becomes a course of action. My organization encourages leadership teams to hold a series of culture-accelerator employee-empowerment workshops to introduce the new operating norms for individuals and teams that will drive innovation, growth, and stellar performance. Teamwork makes the dream work.

The CEO and executive team will have already done this work, so the first wave of employees to go through these workshops should be the next layer of management willing to become ambassadors of the organization's culture. If the change initiative simply lives with the executive team, it falls flat. The CEO can't just send out an email about the company's new mission, vision, and values and expect a shift. People need to be inspired to adopt new thinking and behaviors. They must learn new ways to communicate, relate to one another, and solve problems together. Those leading expansive organizational change must be willing and able to continually breathe life into the possibilities ahead and inspire their people to do the necessary work to make them a reality. The leadership team's words and deeds must demonstrate what the new transformed culture looks like. This is where most companies break down in their change initiatives. They put together a cultural document and ask everyone to follow the new guidelines with no real training, coaching, or guidance to back up their call for change. Real, sustainable change requires significant support. Helping people overcome the past so they can create a new future requires constant guidance. Remember VUCA? It doesn't just disappear because a culture memo went out to the entire organization. Moving from VUCA to consistent trust, new possibilities, and Liberating Structures is a significant human journey that requires oversight, feedback, constant nurturing, and commitment. Helping people think and behave differently is a full-time undertaking. Don't underestimate the effort required, or your changes won't stick.

The executive team should select a group of leaders, managers, and high-impact players who have a deep desire for a better work environment and are willing to be culture catalysts to support positive change inside the organization. This team of aligned leaders will work together daily to instill the noble cause, values, strategic anchors, and thematic goal in the hearts and minds of the collective. This is also the group that must be regularly trained, guided, and coached about how to roll out and implement Liberating Structures that can shape and guide the behavior, interactions, conversations, and actions of their direct reports and the workforce overall. The change must come from the people doing the work, and, for this to happen, the people who they report to need to be all in. History tells us that, if you can get 10 percent of your organization to believe that true change is underway and have them work on the next 20 percent, the rest of the organization will follow. That's what it takes to get to critical mass.

Training during this phase cannot be purely informational; it must be transformational and allow these agents of change to experience what the future *feels* like. The culture kickoff takes these agents of change through a series of inquiries and experiential exercises to experience the new way of working and being. An example might be practicing specific Liberating Structures to see how operating as one human system might work in the real world. This could be done in small groups of 20 to 25 employees to show them how healthy, high-performance teams communicate, operate, and navigate to achieve strategic initiatives and goals. As soon as they're immersed in practice sessions of this new reality, they begin to understand that new levels of communication, discipline, and accountability are required.

In other sessions, the group works to create Liberating Structures to allow team members to interact and communicate more effectively, build and strengthen relationships, and create an environment of trust and alignment in which amazing things can happen. Think of these workshops as culture accelerators filled with practical exercises that show the change agents in your organization how to unleash the human spirit at work. Participants get their first taste of self-actualization at work—and it is *highly* motivating. Each team walks away from these workshops with:

- A deep personal understanding of the organization's noble purpose, vision, and core values.
- A new level of ownership for their own success as well as the team and company's success.

155

- A clearer understanding of what it feels like to stretch beyond one's comfort zone in order to be part of a high-performance team.
- New ways to communicate and interact productively as both individuals and in groups—even when the going gets tough.

These immersive workshops not only inspire people to take ownership of the organization's noble cause, mission, vision, and values; they *show* them how to do it daily. When individuals go through the training in a culture kickoff, they start living the company's values, solving problems, and creating the future together with the company's noble cause in mind. They experience for the first time what dramatic shifts in behavior look and feel like. It's very powerful. This is the beginning of organization-wide alignment, which is necessary for lasting, positive change.

KEY TAKEAWAYS

- Change is a never-ending journey. Everyone needs to keep growing—you, your executive team, and your people.
- In the beginning of any change initiative, the past is ever present. Most people have ideas about the future that are shaped by old self-limiting beliefs and often negative past experiences and contexts. You and your leadership team must help them envision a better future—as you have done for yourselves.
- There are seven disciplines that must be developed to create transformational change: the conscious use of self, systems orientation, openness to sound and current data, constructive feedback, respect for the collective intelligence, learning from differences, and empowerment.

BRAINHACK

Patience comes from impulse control, and your prefrontal cortex drives this function. The executive brain not only coordinates what you do; it also coordinates what you don't do. Sending inhibitory signals to your brain and body is an incredibly important function. In order to be patient, you have to first learn to control your impulses. The best way to do this is by planning your day around your impulses. Start by making a list throughout your day of all the negative influences you act on. Do you check your phone too often? Do you get sidetracked by your email or by the other people in your office? Next, create a plan to aid you in controlling those impulses. Turn off your phone or place it in an inconvenient spot that will take work to retrieve. Close your email tab and sign out of your account so that to check it you would have to sign back in. Move to a quieter part of your office or put in headphones and play non-distracting music. Make it harder for yourself to act on your impulses. Over time, your impulses to do those things will decrease. The less energy your brain must put towards impulse control, the more energy it can have for productivity, creativity, and critical thinking. Set yourself up for success.

POWERFUL QUESTIONS

- What is resonating for you in this chapter?
- How can you and your leadership team help others envision a better future?
- Who are the people that come to mind who can support this change in the most effective positive way?

CHAPTER 12

Getting to Critical Mass

"When an idea reaches critical mass
there is no stopping the shift its presence will induce."

— MARIANNE WILLIAMSON —

To successfully transform an organization's culture, about 10% of the people in the human system need to become agents of change. This means that, if a company has a thousand employees, a hundred of them are evangelizing and modeling new emergent behaviors on a regular basis and encouraging others to do the same. In my organization, we call these people culture catalysts. They become the leadership team's boots on the floor. They have voluntarily taken on a second job to assist in the organization's cultural transformation. They're provided with training, coaching, and guidance in order to do this successfully. Building on the work of this group, pilot programs are created in high-impact areas of the company, or maybe a decision is made to introduce cultural change through cross-functional teams or department by department. No matter how it's done, it's key that the leadership team creates an organization-wide roadmap to unveil the change to everyone.

Operationalizing Culture

Many of you are probably saying, "10 percent seems like a reasonable goal. I'm sure I can get 10 percent of my people to become agents of change. Not a problem." Well, in this case, it might be easier said than done. You see, these people can't just be yes-men (or -women). To be effective agents of change, they must be true believers. They have to want these changes to happen so bad they can taste it. That type of commitment just doesn't happen overnight. In fact, for many people, that type of commitment won't come easily. As we discussed earlier in the book, most people left to their own devices go through the workday on autopilot. You're going to have to snap them out of that zombie-like state if you want real transformational change to start happening.

What if you intentionally interrupted all of your company's day-to-day business operations and called everyone together for an 'all hands' to announce the cultural transformation initiative and explore all the tools, resources, and training that you're going to put in place to support everyone in successfully navigating this change? You could explain that this is about aligning the hearts and minds of the organization to come together and move the noble cause forward. You could share that change begins when the organization's core values are operationalized so everyone can operate at their highest level in a friction-free work environment. When the system is organized in a way that brings out the best in people, fulfillment and self-actualization become the norm.

An important step in building trust is transparency. In order to demonstrate that the change initiative has been embraced at the highest levels of the organization, are you willing to discuss past mistakes and publicly commit to a more human-centered style of leadership that embraces the noble cause, mission, vision, and values that make the company exceptional? Are you willing to explain that you plan to examine the behavioral norms of individuals, teams, management, and so forth—and tell the truth about what you find? Are you open to pledging to be more cognizant of everyone's experience and recognize that a great organization values its people and helps them self-actualize through meaningful work? Do you feel comfortable assuring everyone that you will provide the support, resources, and tools necessary to create a high-performance organization capable of achieving its goals precisely because of a human-centric, emergent culture?

The goal of this significant launch event is to get people to feel the vision for themselves and see their place in it. If you are successful, people will lean in—perhaps hesitantly at first, but they're moving in the right direction. Can you imagine the positive message that such an event sends to everyone? It is in this type of inspiring setting that the first volunteers typically step forward to become agents of change. It's an exciting moment—a new beginning.

Begin with Sound and Current Data

Once you have your changemakers—your culture catalyst team—opting in to support the culture journey, it is important to begin collecting sound and current data with inclusivity, diversity, and engagement top of mind. Rolling out a survey that gives your employees an opportunity to express their version of an ideal culture is an outstanding way to demonstrate that culture is a top priority. These changemakers can socialize the importance of survey participation and candid feedback as well as express the positive consequences of sharing input that can guide the organization's culture now and in the future.

Human Synergistics' Organizational Culture Inventory® (ICO®) suggests an *ideal* culture survey as a great way to learn more about what employees and owners want in and from the organization's culture. Once the survey results are tabulated and socialized by the culture catalyst team, the next step is to launch a follow-up survey about the *actual* culture. This gives organizational leaders sound and current data about the current state of affairs. The results help the leadership team identify strategies for improving culture and

Margaret Graziano

performance. The data offers a clear roadmap to categorize and sequence change initiatives in a way that makes sense—and, if successful, will deliver the best and fastest return on investment. Early wins in closing the gap between ideal and actual culture establish the organization's culture as a real priority. This builds trust and reduces any fears people might have.

Concentric Circles of Support

When organizations begin to scale quickly, more people and processes are necessary to support the accelerated growth. Everyone in business understands this basic principle. Such is the case with cultural transformation as well. As change spreads to more people and teams throughout an organization, the change takes on a momentum of its own. And there must be a growing support system of people and high-level architecture to handle the quickening pace of this change. But, because transformation doesn't fall into a simple business bucket like sales, marketing, technology, or administration, the proper support systems are often not put in place. This is especially risky because a healthy, high-performance culture isn't a destination; it's an ongoing journey. It's generative and calls for maintenance of what's working and destruction of anything that's getting in the way of progress—like all the old behaviors that had prevented growth in the past. Without a system in place to support this virtuous cycle, the journey quickly becomes unsustainable. Positive change becomes less frequent. People go from inspired to frustrated and complacent. There might even be some regression. This can happen quite quickly, which is why solid support systems need to be in place *before* the cultural transformation is even announced. If ongoing change and growth aren't fully supported, it's actually easier for everyone to slide backward into old habits than continue pushing forward into a new and transformative way of working. It's a major challenge, and, when people are working in a

162

high-performance environment, leaders need to ensure that it's also a high-support environment. There can be no exceptions to this rule if you wish to be successful.

Unfortunately, culture initiatives tend to get rushed. People are busy. They have other priorities. The quick fix at many organizations is to hire someone to manage all the ongoing change. These positions have various names: vice president of people or director of change or head of human resources, to name a few. Most of the time, this person has never been in charge of a cultural transformation. This is a big, and surprisingly common, mistake. The people put in these positions are often process or structure experts who don't always put people first. Sadly, they often end up being part of the problem, not the solution. This is why the CEO and executive team that created the original vision for cultural transformation must stay at the helm and surround themselves with supporters who are fully aligned with their vision. These are groups of people to whom the CEO and executive team can allocate work, rely upon to improve communication throughout their part of the organization, and count on to create and support Liberating Structures that align and empower the people who report to them. That group, in turn, needs its own support group, and so on.

Rather than a hierarchy, think of this model of change management as a series of concentric support circles. Each support circle is only as strong as the circle before it, so there must be continuous measurement, communication, and feedback to make sure this structure stays strong. This model is the only way for an organization to continue its journey of improvement and achievement. If you want your company to be a market leader, you need to stay on the journey. If you want to stay on the journey, you need to be constantly enriching your human system's ability to motivate, collaborate, and innovate. This can only be achieved in proactive, emergent cultures, which need constant support and nurturing. Keeping an entire organization aligned around your company's noble cause, vision, mission, and values is no easy feat. But whichever company does this best and most effectively wins.

Change Churn

When it comes to change, leaders must accept that adoption is a constant two-steps-forward, one-step-back effort. It's sort of like churn in a SaaS business. You have new subscribers each month, but there are those who opt out and bring down the net user-growth numbers. Make sense? There will always be naysayers during cultural transformation. The pull to keep things as they have always been never fully disappears. There is always going to be what we call "change churn." As the transformation gets further along, this will be less of a problem. But, in the beginning, when you only have a small group of change agents evangelizing for cultural transformation, the naysayers can really weigh down progress. A strong support system can reduce change churn, but many leadership teams underestimate the scope of support required. Don't reach for bandages—like mindless perks, beer, ping pong, and "rah-rah" events—none of which fosters real change.

The majority of CEOs I talk to—and I've talked to thousands—proudly tell me they lead high-challenge work environments. But, when I ask them how they support the people trying to keep their head above water in that type of environment, most go silent. And still they wonder why their employees are struggling, calling in sick, or leaving the company. It's a mystery to me that most leaders don't see the correlation. When people aren't properly supported, they can't work at their highest level, and they can't take on new things like cultural transformation. They're just trying to survive. The only way a CEO can get to the heart of this problem is to gather people together regularly and ask, "What tools and resources do you need to manage ongoing change and growth effectively?" Give people a say in the process. This is empowering in and of itself. Let everyone play a role in solving problems and dismantling the roadblocks that stand in the way of positive change. Listen closely to their feedback. They know what they need to process and adapt to change in a high-challenge environment. The support they need can come in many forms. It might be more training, better onboarding, added coaching, professional and personal development resources, outsourcing or insourcing to reassign certain tasks, technology development to automate certain processes, or something else. It could even mean a reengineered work week that offers more time for creativity and restoration to lift spirits and open minds—both of which are required for innovation.

Be open to all of their ideas. Think about what's possible and provide your people with whatever it takes to help them stay on the cultural transformation journey. It's worth the time, money, and effort. The future of your company is at stake. If you can't reach critical mass for your cultural transformation initiatives, the future looks bleak. If the majority of your people aren't fully onboard with the new behaviors, attitudes, and ways of doing things, there will be a heavy drag on your organization's forward momentum. This means that, when your leadership team introduces new strategies, they won't gain traction quickly. They may even fall flat. As legendary management consultant Peter Drucker once said, "Culture eats strategy for breakfast." So true! Align your culture and watch your organization soar.

Snuff Out VUCA

We are currently living in one of the most volatile, uncertain, complex, and ambiguous times in human history. The world is moving faster than ever, and organizations that aren't leading their markets are falling behind faster than ever. These rapid changes demand exceptional teamwork, innovation, and motivation. Any organization seeking to compete without all three of these superpowers built into the fabric of their company culture is at a huge competitive disadvantage. The ability to respond to change rapidly has never been more important. Change is easier when a culture embraces it as part of the daily routine, which is not how most companies operate today.

The number-one reason change initiatives fail is because entrenched behaviors from the past aren't snuffed out. These toxic patterns can linger at the executive leadership level or lower-management levels. Either way, the VUCA slips back into daily business and undermines change. This happens because there's not a solid support system in place to nurture the virtuous cycle of creation, maintenance, and destruction necessary to support the never-ending journey of growth in a high-performance culture.

I see this problem often. It's disappointing to watch. I coached a CEO named Harry for about two years. In many ways, he was the model coachee—always on time, prepared, seemingly eager to move forward in his personal and professional development, and willing to try the tools I provided. Early on in our coaching engagement, he tried to bring various change efforts to his organization. Each was met with nitpicking, resistance, doubt, and reticence. Unfortunately, Harry hadn't yet mastered the art and science of navigating his internal saboteurs. Not only did his company need support systems to sustain the change, but Harry also needed them as the CEO. He had a big blind spot around being liked by his people. As a result, he only took risks that wouldn't ruffle too many feathers. All too often, this meant he backtracked when change initiatives became challenging—as they always do. It also meant that he left organizational time bombs ticking all over the place. Additionally, Harry and his executive team's adrenaline bias caused them to adopt quick solutions to important problems that needed deeper consideration. It was a toxic combination that was leading to big problems.

During our coaching sessions, I could actually see Harry's expression change as he experienced "ah-ha" moments when we he discovered that his company's resistance to change began and ended with him. He left our sessions with the best intentions, eager to do the right thing. But, without the proper framework and support systems in place on his executive team, those moments didn't translate into behavioral changes in the work environment. Since nothing was changing at the root level, the ticking time bombs started exploding all over the place. People were confused by a lack of commitment and clear direction from their executive team. While the organization was on an all-time growth high, things began to fall apart, and long-time inventory problems got worse. A lack of process and systems around how sales were made was causing friction up and down the chain. Revenue was rising, yet the cost of doing business was accelerating faster. The departure of key talent meant historical knowledge was shrinking, and technology was used because people had to use it, which caused rampant company-wide waste. The company was burning through cash. It was only a matter of time before the damage would become irreversible. Harry knew the future wouldn't be kind to the company if he didn't muster up the grit and determination to make it happen.

He began to meditate and visualize himself as the leader who guides a company forward. Through rigorous self-development, asking for feedback, and practicing focusing his mind, he began to see where he was getting in his own way. He practiced conversations for action before he met with members of his executive team. He used breakdowns as an opportunity to build trust. He was well aware that he needed to slow down and devote a considerable amount of energy to creating a stronger foundation to support more sustainable change—including continuing to change his own behavior. Harry is now well on his journey. Early on this new path, he pulled me aside and said, "I get it now. I cannot spend or outsource my way to effective, sustainable change; we all must walk through it, step by step. We need to have each other's back and keep our commitments. I see it now—this is the long game"

Don't fall into the trap Harry was in for so long. Give yourself and your people the support they need. Like Harry's company, many organizations that undertake transformative cultural change are starting from a less-than-optimal place. All too many companies operate from either too much management—the command-and-control approach—or too little leadership—decision by consensus—both of which can become mired in interpersonal entanglement, leading to people being exasperated, exhausted, overwhelmed, and frustrated.

Additionally, people bring all of their own baggage to work. It can be a toxic combination, but it's the human condition—and the mounting chaos of modern life doesn't lighten the load on people. Everyone is walking around with wounds and stress. No one can think through new ideas effectively when in such a state. Then, you and your leadership team march in and introduce a host of exciting new changes. You're all pumped up. But, as you bring your message of hope and an exciting new future to the masses, you find you're not preaching to the choir. In fact, people just shrug. They don't have the energy for change. Don't let this surprise you. It's normal. The knee-jerk reaction from most employees will be that all this change is going to make their lives tougher for a while. Fears arise because change triggers every insecurity we have. *Do I have what it takes to live up to the new behaviors? Is this for real? Will these changes actually stick? Is my boss really going to stop being so toxic? If I speak up, will I be labeled a troublemaker, as I have been in the past? Is my workday really going to get better? How long will this take? How much time am I going to have to devote to this? I'm already so busy.* The leadership team must not underestimate the resistance they'll encounter, especially in the beginning. People's feelings and experiences with entrenched toxic behaviors won't just magically disappear. Relationships and people need time to heal. People's moods around change all too often cause natural resistance. That's why they need as much proactive support as can be provided—more even than the people they're trying to help. When leading people to be their highest and best self at work and in life, Jeff Willmore, co-founder of the Autonomy Course, encourages his students to become master mood shifters and not fall prey to the thousands of mood derailers tugging for our resources and attention.

As I mentioned, for positive change to stick, you need engagement from your people. Start with those early adopters—that crucial 10 percent. If they feel that they can find fulfillment on your payroll—that they have the opportunity to experience self-actualization in their role and as a result of working with your company—they will stay committed to the cause. They'll bring their entire being to the effort and promote the change your organization needs. But this initial support won't last, and they won't stay on this important journey, if they aren't appropriately supported—both as individuals and agents of change. Do not underestimate the scope or importance of that foundation.

No one can expect employees to simply wake up one day and say, "Hey, my boss said everything's going to be different from here on out. I worked 60 hours last week and have a ton of extra work on my plate already, but count me in!" No one can expect everyone to embrace extreme ownership of a new way of being and doing things when they don't yet fully believe in or understand the cultural transformation and are currently struggling in a less-than-optimal work environment. As we've already discussed, changing hearts and minds requires more than inspirational talks; it requires training, coaching, support, strong communication, feedback, and an environment of trust. People must be heard, supported, and reminded of what's important and where to focus their attention. With all the diversions and attention thieves (think VUCA again), this needs to become part of how the organization operates.

If you want your key agents of change to stay on this important journey and get the most out of it, you need to include them in the shaping of thematic goals and measurements of success. This is the type of work we do in our compelling future workshops. We help teams align around the most important next steps to move the noble cause forward. Quite often, before a team is fully ready to engage in this type of workshop, they need to identify and manage their own preconceived notions and moods around learning, change initiatives, problem solving, and working on teams. Through years of trial and error, my organization has learned that the leadership team needs to experience deep alignment before formulating strategy. Without this step, all too often, we see an organization's strategies fail. In these immersion experiences, these key players have the unique opportunity to inquire into who they are as leaders and create their leadership vision. Much of this journey is about self-awareness, self-discovery, and personal responsibility. They take a close look in the mirror so they can address their own baggage and examine the ingrained patterns and behaviors they bring to work each day. Often, they discover behaviors that are holding them back and causing friction in their work relationships. We help them learn to listen more deeply and communicate more authentically and empathetically. We help them learn how to problem solve productively and without the childish emotions that are often triggered when opinions differ. Think of all the personal and interpersonal work you and your executive team have done to get to this point in your cultural transformation journey. In order to be capable of significant change, your people need to do this work too. Deep alignment immersion experiences help people rebuild trust in one another by bringing them together in a transparent, compassionate, and safe environment where they can tell the truth about what's not working in an empowering, respectful, and constructive way: "We don't say how we're really feeling on this team," or "Why are we holding on to poor performers?" or "Why is it taking thirty hours to get these reports done?"

When we don't honestly articulate what's not working in the enterprise, it leads to a culture of "cordial hypocrisy"—or, as Patrick Lencioni calls it, "artificial harmony." Everyone politely nods in agreement at meetings only to leave and bash the whole plan. That type of toxic behavior isn't going to take your company anywhere meaningful. You've got to eradicate cordial hypocrisy. People need to see and redirect their everyday patterns—worrying, complaining, blaming. They need to understand their impact on the whole and do the internal work to proactively shift their unproductive moods and behaviors so they stop creating discord and waste. Things have to get real before they can change. A cultural reset allows all the humans in your human system to build a new, stronger foundation to support true transformation.

Only when people trust each other and can work together effectively is it time to take your organization to the next level of transformation. Engaging people in a whole new possibility for the enterprise will be short lived if it happens on top of a pile of broken agreements, past upsets, and incompletions. Once the slate is clean, you can start building something new, better, and stronger. This is what changing a culture from the inside out looks like. In truth, it's the *only* way to achieve significant, sustainable change. It takes considerable grit, determination, and time.

To become a market leader, you and your organization must learn how to unleash the human spirit at work—to truly *Ignite Culture!* This is how deep alignment and emergent behaviors begin. In this type of high-challenge, high-support environment, each human being is free to fully contribute their unique talents for the success of the whole. When the individuals in the human system move from divergent agendas and operating styles to congruent behaviors and a shared vision, teamwork thrives. People begin operating in their genius zone and align around the organization's compelling, noble cause. The result is unrivaled innovation.

KEY TAKEAWAYS

- To successfully transform an organization's culture, about 10 percent of its the people in the human system need to become agents of change.
- As change spreads to more people and teams throughout an organization, the change takes on a momentum of its own. And there must be a growing support system of people and high-level architecture to support the quickening pace of this change.
- A strong support system can reduce "change churn," but many leadership teams underestimate the scope of support necessary to sustain ongoing cultural transformation.
- Changing hearts and minds requires more than inspirational talks; it requires training, coaching, support, strong communication, feedback, and an environment of trust. People must be heard, supported, and reminded of what's important and where to focus their attention.

BRAINHACK

Being aware and mindful of our senses activates our prefrontal cortex and helps us regulate stress and stay more present. If you find yourself scattered and not in the moment, try this drill to bring yourself back. Sit up straight with your feet flat on the ground. Start by naming four things that you can see. These can be anything from light, objects, people, or spaces. Next, name three things you physically feel. Do you feel your feet on the ground? Your back against the chair? Become aware of where your body is in space. After that, name two things that you can hear. Really listen to your surroundings and distinguish the sounds coming in. Lastly, label the emotion that you're feeling in the present moment with as much description as you can. Notice how you feel. Are you more present? Repeat this exercise anytime and anywhere until you feel grounded, naming different things every time.

POWERFUL QUESTIONS

- What is resonating for you in this chapter?
- Your leadership presence is needed now more than ever. What's one core value you will intentionally demonstrate to ignite and align your team?
- How would you use generative future based language to change how you communicate your goals to your leadership team?
- Are you ready to do the work to lead an emergent culture?
- What doubts do you notice about you that you need to let go of so you can move forward with your change initiatives and progress in service of your noble cause?

CHAPTER 13

Aligning the Collective Intelligence of a Human System

*"Collective Intelligence (CI) is the capacity of human collectives
to engage in intellectual cooperation in order
to create, innovate, and invent."*

—— PIERRE LEVY ——

When people make an intentional decision to leave behind hopelessness, fear, and frustration in order to bring their best selves to work each day, amazing things begin to happen. The collective positive effect is, as I've said before, larger than the sum of its parts. First, the group steps into a place of courage. They begin to trust in the possibility of a better future and show a willingness to confront negative behaviors that prevent them from realizing that future. Courage is a fragile state, yet, if the group is properly nurtured and supported, the human system enters an even higher level of effectiveness: engagement. In this phase, people focus more on their collective assets and strengths than their individual limitations. People start behaving differently, more constructively and productively. They respect one another and listen more deeply. When people feel heard, they feel valued. When people feel valued, performance and engagement improve dramatically. They enjoy their work and their colleagues. The positive energy becomes palpable, elevating productivity and encouraging ownership. At the two highest levels, innovation accelerates because people set aside their egos, personal agendas, and perceived restrictions to seek the most effective solution to the problem or goal. Then, finally, synchronicity is possible. People want to create positive experiences for everyone in the human system. They see possibility in every challenge and success.

The journey I've just described demonstrates the seven levels of personal group and organizational effectiveness. We will dive deeper into them later in the section in chapter 14, but the immediate question is how does that kind of transformation happen? It sounds miraculous. In truth, this is simply how effective, healthy human systems work when they are nurtured. As people master the skills necessary to move up through the seven levels, the organization's power dynamic shifts dramatically. People move from "*power-over* (directive, dictatorial, dominating, controlling, and often oppressive)" and "*power-against* (win-lose, competitive, conflictual, and often hostile)" to a place where collective intelligence is valued and aligned—"*power-with* (win-win, collaborative, integrative, and often synergic)." These terms were coined by James and Marguerite Craig in their book *Synergic Power* many decades ago. However, they came to be recognized and widely accepted concepts as the field of organizational psychology grew and spread from academic research to real-world management training and coaching. Michael F. Broom, Ph.D., cites these power structures in his book *The Infinite Organization*, which celebrates the positive use of power in human systems. As an executive coach, facilitator, consultant, educator, and author who studies the dynamics of power within human systems, Broom offers a path from personal to organizational power. And, contrary to the popular notion that power is held by a select few, Broom believes power is unlimited when you partner and learn from others.

Broom's philosophy of "infinite power" is one my organization embraces. When we run cultural alignment breakthrough programs with organizations, we see infinite power unfold in front of our eyes. Once people get a taste of what it's like to work together at a higher and deeper level, they're shocked when they reflect on the destructive entrenched behaviors that they had accepted as normal for so long. They now fully understand how these behaviors have derailed strategies and disrupted productivity in the past. People often become very emotional as these light-bulb moments occur. We watch them hugging, crying, and apologizing to one another for poor behavior, acting out, letting their team members down, and more. It's a clearing of the slate, a brand-new beginning, a complete reset—and it's always filled with hope and promise.

When leaders focus on their organization as a human system with infinite power, Broom explains that it's critical to understand the importance of creating solutions that:

- Do not cause other problems
- Prevent the same problems from occurring again
- Support all parts of the larger system

"When human systems work," Broom states, "all other systems work better." That's a very important idea. It's my experience that most leaders believe it's the other way around, but it's not. The human system is where the focus must be. All else flows from its overall health and effectiveness.

Characteristics of Human Systems

With the above in mind, Broom's characteristics of human systems are worthy of your attention. This straightforward list makes it crystal clear what is needed as you navigate the unknown and sometimes treacherous waters of cultural transformation. It's a list you should keep close at hand. According to Broom:

1. Goal achievement is the primary purpose of any system. Clarity is paramount for effectiveness.
2. Alignment of system members is a primary strategy for goal achievement that, without alignment, tends to take the form of suppression of differences (conformity) or other win/lose power dynamics (power struggles, turf battles) rather than collaborative, win/win, synergetic dynamics.
3. Feedback loops regulate the behavior of systems and keep the system on target toward its goals. Performance data, rewards, penalties, and permissions are examples of feedback.
4. The effectiveness of human systems over time is proportional to the quality of the relationships within the system. Trust and mutual understanding are indicators of high-quality relationships.
5. A problematic human system will mitigate the effectiveness of related human, mechanical, or electronic systems. Failure to frequently attend to the quality of a human system is costly in terms of effectiveness and efficiency.

6. For a system to be doing what it's doing, everyone in that system must be doing what they're doing. Accordingly, responsibility is always mutual—everyone is to be credited, and everyone is to be blamed. Everyone impacts the system, and the system impacts everyone.
7. Any member of a system will consistently succeed (or fail) only with the support of the system.
8. The behavior of leaders (as collectively interpreted by followers) has a significant impact on the behavior (collaboration, competition, conformity, anarchy) that occurs within human systems.
9. The members of systems are diverse. Innovation is dependent on the effective use of diversity. At the same time, the preponderance of problematic human systems stems from differences (diversity) being squashed into conformity or used for hostility and contention.
10. Human-system problems are often better dealt with through improving relationships (trust and mutual understanding) among the system's members rather than removing/replacing members. This requires being curious about what's going on rather than judging those involved. After all, you too are a part of that system.
11. Managing change in human systems requires seeing ourselves as part of the system, understanding our impact on the system at hand, and modifying our behavior as needed.

Authors Solomon and Flores reinforce the profound role of trust in their book *Building Trust*:

> Corporate seminars and workshops stress all sorts of skills and motivational attitudes. But what makes most companies falter—leaving aside market forces, bad products, and incompetent management— is the lack of trust. Employees don't trust their

supervisors or managers. They may not even trust one another. Mangers practice cordial hypocrisy as a matter of course, and consequently, even if they like one another, they do not trust one another (but often confuse the two). Top executives, at least among themselves, may play a subtler and rougher game. Nevertheless, the companies that function best are almost always those that have trust and harmony at the top, emanating through the organization.

Broom believes that small groups are the fundamental unit of human systems. They are where authentic trust is built. I agree. When Jeff Bezos was CEO of Amazon, he famously touted the benefits of the "two pizza team." In his opinion, if a team couldn't be fed with two pizzas, it was too big. In a 2013 letter to shareholders, Bezos highlighted how having smaller, decentralized teams helped Amazon spur creativity and innovation: "This decentralized distribution of invention throughout the company—not limited to the company's senior leaders—is the only way to get robust, high-throughput innovation." When it comes to small groups, Bezos and Broom share similar beliefs. Broom says small groups work best when:

1. The members of the team are interdependent of one another for the successful accomplishment of its goals.
2. Membership is five to ten people who consistently and routinely help and support one another.
3. The leaders have a clear place to go and people willing to follow.
4. Team members believe their leaders genuinely care—i.e., genuinely express interest in, curiosity about, and appreciation of both the team and each of its members.
5. Power dynamics are such that members are willing to learn from their differences to create innovation and synergy and to avoid the waste of undue contention or suppression.

6. Trust and the assumption of good intentions have been well developed through the effective management of human processes, such as dialogic communication, learning from differences, feedback, and conflict management.
7. Dialogic feedback that is team based and supportive is routinely used to keep the team and its individual members on course.
8. The team as a whole is rewarded (or penalized) for its successes, and the team rewards (or penalizes) its individual members.

Small groups are the most effective way to ignite change quickly. If you can get a small team to work well together, you have a model to show others. That can be powerful. This is how we worked with a 140-year-old manufacturing company based in Iowa. It was a three-year engagement. The organization was in deep trouble and in serious need of an intervention. The us-versus-them mentality had taken the company's dysfunction to new heights and manifested in lawsuits, increased safety violations, and hostile union negotiations. Things were unraveling fast. Downtime was increasing, sick leave was at an all-time high, and production numbers were the worst they had been in more than a decade. We were brought in by the executive team to turn their toxic culture around. After several months of working with multiple levels of personnel—from foremen and forklift drivers to executives and accounting clerks—a collective of 120 out of 400 employees volunteered to become change agents. A small group of front-line supervisors committed to working together to tighten up how people were hired and onboarded. A small group from quality control stepped up to improve processes and reporting. There were small teams working on all sorts of important change—from helping managers become better delegators to improving processes and inspiring people to work more collaboratively. In twelve months, there were thirty-six operational and HR initiatives and process improvements completed. Surveys about employee experience jumped from 2.5 out of 5 points to 4.2. Change was happening, and it was across the company's entire human system. People felt like they were part of something big and important as they started to create change together for the first time in many decades. During the time we were working with this company, profits also increased by eight points, significantly improving the bottom line.

KEY TAKEAWAYS

- "When human systems work," Michael F. Broom states, "all other systems work better." If you want to facilitate lasting transformational change, work on your human systems.
- When people feel heard, they feel valued. When people feel valued, performance and engagement improve dramatically. They enjoy their work and their colleagues.
- As Amazon's Jeff Bezos advises, smaller, decentralized teams help spur creativity and innovation: "This decentralized distribution of invention throughout the company—not limited to the company's senior leaders—is the only way to get robust, high-throughput innovation." Small groups are the most effective way to ignite change quickly.

BRAINHACK

The cerebellum is the part of your brain that coordinates complex movements and coordination and eliminates all unwanted movement, thoughts, and emotions. If you want to increase your response agility and decrease the number of unwanted reactions you have, try this drill to stimulate the cerebellum. Sit or stand straight up with your feet on the ground. Start with your non-dominant hand and rotate your wrist in a figure-8 pattern five times. Then rotate that same wrist five times going the opposite direction. Do the same thing with your dominant hand, rotating it in a figure-8 pattern five times one way and five times the other. Doing this will upregulate your cerebellum and aid you in getting rid of unwanted thoughts, feelings, and reactions. The more times a day you do this, the better the results will be.

POWERFUL QUESTIONS

- What is resonating for you in this chapter?
- What adjectives would you use to describe the human system at your company?
- What is your company doing that strengthens the human systems' ability to build trust and facilitate effective conversations for action and workflow that lead to effective, efficient, and successful outcomes?

CHAPTER 14

The Transformative Energy of a Self-Actualized Culture

"Make sure everybody in the company has great opportunities, has a meaningful impact and is contributing to the good of society."

— LARRY PAGE —

T he Great Resignation signals that there are too many toxic cultures populating corporate America. Employees feel scared, ignored, overlooked, and undervalued. In such environments, people keep their heads down and just try to survive. It's a terrible waste of human potential and one of the biggest reasons people are leaving their jobs. They are unfulfilled, unhappy, and often unhealthy as a result of all the stress and bad behavior they have to deal with at work. However, if the CEO and leadership team are committed toputting in the effort to turn things around, transformation *is* possible. People can go from merely surviving to abundantly thriving. When people feel safe, welcome, inspired, and valued in their jobs, they bring their hearts to work and contribute meaningfully.

So, what kind of experience are people having at your organization?

Let's look at the employee experience from the start—hiring and onboarding. The doorway to culture begins with hiring. Your company must be attracting and recruiting the *right* people—those aligned with your noble cause, mission, vision, and values. Top employees look for meaningful work at purposeful companies. If the word on the street is that your company has a noble mission, clear values, and a healthy work environment where employees can thrive, then you probably have an advantage over many companies in your industry. Job seekers want to know that your culture is more than corporate speak. They want to see leadership walking the talk. Today, former employees can share their experiences at companies very publicly, so there's a lot of information for job seekers to review to see if what you say about your culture in your recruiting materials is actually real or not. I've said it before, and I'll say it again: you can't fake culture. You can't half-ass it. Culture isn't some initiative that can be handed over to human resources. The CEO, leadership team, HR, and your employees have to be "all in," as Chester Elton writes in his book *All In: How the Best Managers Create a Culture of Belief and Drive Big Results,* co-authored by Adrian Gostick:

> If your culture is clear, positive, and strong, then your people will buy into your ideas and cause and, most important, will believe what they do matters and that they can make a difference. That pervasive enthusiasm and energy will spread. . . . On the other hand, if your culture is dysfunctional— chaotic, combative, or indifferent—employees will most likely spend more time thinking about why the people sitting next to them should be fired than getting fired up themselves.

If your people are fired up, your company will be well positioned to attract and hire more of the right people. If they're not, it's going to show up all over the internet, and your recruiting efforts will be doomed. The right people will click away before you ever even discover they're interested in your job listing. In today's competitive hiring market, this is a big problem. In my organization, we show leadership teams how to create an effective talent optimization strategy that infuses the organization's culture into every step of the employee lifecycle. We're big fans of Steven Cox's approach and his eight-phase diversity-and-inclusion employee lifecycle but with a culture layer. Cox is a leading UK-based executive leadership coach and advisor. Here's his approach with my twist:

1. **Strategy.** A company's people deliver its strategy. Know what types of people and skills your company needs and where. It's key to an effective people strategy. *My twist:* Infuse your people strategy with strong cultural elements that reflect your organization's noble cause and core values. Build the "why" into this experience and connect to the hearts and heads of your people.

2. **Attraction.** Attracting the best people is about corporate reputation. Make sure the information potential candidates hear and read about your company encourages the best people to apply. *My twist:* When your organization's reputation is based on a noble cause and core values, it will attract candidates aligned with your self-actualized culture. Remember, candidates will need to understand how their role will provide a pathway to self-actualization. Every role needs a clear purpose that is aligned with the company's noble cause, mission, vision, and values. The intersection of meaningful work serving a noble cause combined with growth that aligns with personal goals and career ambitions is what attracts and retains the best people for a high-performance company.

3. **Recruitment.** Your recruitment process must be free of bias and clearly signal your company's interest in diverse candidates. Set high expectations in this area for your recruiting managers and agencies. *My twist:* Recruit and hire diverse candidates. According to McKinsey, companies that focus on gender diversity on their executive teams were 21 percent more likely to experience above-average profitability, and companies focused on ethnic diversity saw a 33 percent likelihood of outperformance on margin. Diversity and inclusion are important core organizational values that should be incorporated into the entire employee lifecycle. Create clear, straightforward hiring standards before you start recruiting and ensure each and every candidate is evaluated for their passion for the organization, desire to do the work required, capability in the desired role, affinity for and deep resonance with the organization's noble cause, and behavioral alignment with its core values.

4. **Onboarding.** This is an opportunity for new employees to understand expectations, gain training and support, and learn about opportunities available to them. *My twist:* Onboarding is also an excellent time to articulate the company's noble cause, mission, vision and values and demonstrate how they shape positive behavior and a healthy, productive culture for all employees. This is where the rubber hits the road. Showing new employees how the organization's noble cause manifests in daily activities demonstrates integrity. The truth is employees typically look for other jobs up to six months after they start just in case the job they are in doesn't live up to expectations. You need to show them why they should stop looking.

5. **Growth and Development.** Learning and training should always provide diversity and inclusion opportunities and voices.

My twist: Learning, development, and training should have strong cultural overtones that incorporate the company's noble cause, mission, vision and values. Does the organization have the Liberating Structures in place to allow employees to resolve issues, communicate effectively, and be true contributors so they can experience self-actualization in a group environment? An organization with a high-performance culture trains frequently on this and makes learning a core tenet of the employment experience.

6. **Rewards and Recognition.** All employees must be treated equitably. Benefits should be inclusive. *My twist:* Rewards, recognition, and benefits can't be superficial. There's too much of that in corporate America today. Instead, rewards, recognition, and benefits need to be meaningful and closely aligned with the company's core values, noble cause, thematic goals, and success measures.

7. **Promotion and Measurement.** Work allocation and performance management should be consistent and equitable. *My twist:* Performance and behaviors that align with the company's core values must be rewarded and reinforced. Tangible ways to reinforce and reward core-value alignment include assigning new elevated opportunities to grow and stretch, acknowledgement for very specific actions and outcomes, and consideration for promotion into management roles where transparency and organizational alignment are required. Performance and behaviors that aren't aligned with the company's core values should be continuously assessed and addressed with cultural and behavioral training, coaching, mentoring, and immersive workshops.

8. **Retaining.** Talent of all types should want to stay with the company. The leadership team needs to act upon

feedback and promote workplace inclusion and diversity programs. *My twist:* If employees are able to thrive, grow, and self-actualize at work, employee turnover should be below average. The loss of an employee should always present an opportunity to assess and strengthen the organization's culture.

When the organization's noble cause, mission, and values are integrated into every step of the employee experience, then alignment, achievement, and self-actualization take center stage. Even performance is measured and rewarded differently. If a team isn't performing well, the question isn't whether the manager running that team is good or not, or even whether he or she is hitting KPIs. Instead, the question becomes whether the manager believes in the organization's noble cause, is fully committed to its vision, respects its core values, and is operating in alignment with the agreed-upon thematic goals, priorities, and areas of accountability. If there's a mismatch in any of these areas, then the person shouldn't stay—actually, they shouldn't have been brought into the organization in the first place. Infusing culture into recruiting and onboarding is a proactive way to address this issue.

Onboarding and training on diverse communication styles, healthy and smart organizational culture, effective conflict resolution, and proactive, collaborative problem solving, as well as the how-tos of operationalizing core values and subsequent behaviors on the job, are all hallmarks of high-performance organizations with strong cultures. The goal is to enrich the company's human system with open, fluid communication and curiosity. When this is the norm in organizations, VUCA, which is a proven showstopper, no longer has the power to derail strategy. This is where training managers on the transformative power of Liberating Structures can be, well, quite liberating. These structures empower people to replace VUCA with clarity, continuity, ease, and flow. This changes everyone's day-to-day work experience and interactions. This builds authentic trust. It opens a gateway to exceptional teamwork and collaboration, unrivaled innovation, intrinsic motivation, authentic contribution, and self-actualization.

Simon's VUCA Problem

"Magi, we're doing it all!" As the leader of a fast-growing tech company on the West Coast, CEO Simon Hoffstatter was perplexed. He had hired me to help his company improve its talent retention and acquisition. "We offer great benefits, 10 percent higher pay than our competitors, unlimited time off, foosball, racquetball, and remote work. We even have lunch delivered twice a week to the whole company!"

"I understand, Simon," I said, nodding my head. "You're doing a lot of things right. For goodness sakes, you've grown 75 percent three years in a row. That's impressive. But I'm being told over and over by your people that the leadership team isn't on the same page and that management doesn't understand their pain points. There's also a lot of VUCA here. You are . . ."

"Magi," Simon interrupted, exasperation in his voice. "I'm exhausted every day trying to resolve all the problems. The leadership team is trying to send the right message about the important work we're doing here—our noble cause. But I feel like there's a breakdown. People say they'll get the job done, and they don't, so then I have to step in. There aren't enough hours in the day!"

"You're right. There is a breakdown," I told Simon. "You're growing really fast, and everyone's just trying to keep their head above water. You offer a lot of perks, but what you're not offering is time for your employees. They're stressed out, overwhelmed, under supported, and often confused about expectations and roles. What's missing is a humanistic, affiliative, self-actualized culture where they can collaborate, solve their own problems, and thrive. That's why they're underperforming and leaving. And, unfortunately, word is spreading, so it's becoming much more challenging for you to attract the new talent that you need to grow your business. I encourage you to make this problem a top priority, Simon. Fixing it is central to your company's ongoing success."

Simon's company was spending all its money on stuff to try to make people happy, but it wasn't generating the results he wanted. What his people had been asking for was more time to get up to speed after being hired or asked to take on a new role. They wanted clearer and more consistent communication, one on ones with their managers to answer questions, and more training. Simon had an engagement issue. People were either quitting or not performing the way that the company needed them to perform in order to become a market leader. Additionally, his managers hadn't been trained properly on how to lead, allocate work, or relate to people effectively in alignment with the company's noble cause, mission, vision and values. They needed to learn how to build stronger relationships with their people and get rid of ingrained habits and routines so employees stopped feeling like cogs in the wheel.

Simon had an entangled, gridlocked culture that was preventing rapid implementation of the organization's best strategies and most powerful ideas. It was also causing a talent problem. All of this was limiting growth and making it extremely challenging to keep pace with market changes. Simon just kept pushing people harder and harder to reach the next milestone, and people were just burned out. Yes, his company was growing fast, but he would need even faster growth to become the market leader. But entanglement and VUCA were causing gridlock and limiting the company's potential.

Signs of Gridlock

Over the years, I've had the opportunity to work in many different types of cultures—some healthier than others. But I've developed a sort of sixth sense for gridlocked cultures. I can spot them almost as soon as I start working with a company. Here are a few warning signs that you might have a gridlocked culture:

- New ideas cause a combination of infighting, side taking, nitpicking, and responsibility avoidance. Uninspired people are just working to survive, so, when a new idea is introduced, they do the absolute minimum they need to do to keep their job.
- It takes a long time to make decisions and even longer to implement them—that's if they're even implemented at all.
- There are people in the organization who say yes to nearly everything but don't follow through—at least not to the degree they committed.
- There are many rules within the organization that are selectively enforced or often allowed to slide.
- There is almost no agreement on the company's values. Everyone values different things.
- There isn't a single, uniting noble cause that has been agreed upon, focused upon, or acted upon.
- People's personal and positional agendas are often leading their decisions and actions.
- There's an incredible amount of potential and talent within the organization that's being wasted and underutilized.
- Many people are conforming and avoiding rather than engaging and performing.
- Many people across the organization believe secrets are being kept from them. The paranoia is palpable.

If you're seeing a few of these warning signs in your organization, it's time to make a change. A cultural intervention might be the best next step, or an open forum discussion group about the current state of the organizational culture might be another, or another first step might be to lean into data collection and roll out an ideal/actual culture survey highlighting what people are longing for inside their workplace culture as compared to what they are currently experiencing. For some, this is a tough pill to swallow. The data is clear and honest and gives direct feedback on how well the executive leadership and management team are or aren't walking the talk when it comes to a healthy culture. Without intervention, toxic behaviors and mindsets will eventually drag down or hold back your company—probably sooner than you think.

Keep the Covenant

If you want people to bring their hearts and minds to work so that they can fully contribute and enrich your company's human system, then you, your leadership team, and your managers all must learn and employ more effective communication and interaction skills and build deeper trust at every level in the organization. That's how you help your people and retain them. Only when these things are in place can you start giving rewards and recognition, because then they have some meaning.

If you want leaders and managers to tap into people's highest level of intelligence, they need to learn to understand their people's drivers, why they said yes to the job, and their vision for their career. These things must be explored in an atmosphere of trust and respect. Liberating Structures need to be put in place with plenty of regular training and role playing to show both veteran and new employees as well as managers how these structures work and how to use them effectively in the everyday work environment. This is how an organization's human system moves from routine to genius. This is when you can lean in and say to a team, "Partner with me to move this vision forward." In this type of environment, people won't just nod their heads in cordial hypocrisy; they'll actually follow through on their promises and go above and beyond without being asked. They'll get more done with less effort and fix systemic problems rather than apply bandages that eventually distract focus and cripple productivity.

If you want this type of commitment and drive, there's a covenant you can't break: when people say yes to an organization for the right reason, you must honor that trust. You can't deliver VUCA and gridlock; you must deliver on the promise made during the recruiting and onboarding process. You have to stay true to your culture journey and continually create, nurture, and protect the healthy, humanistic culture that's allowing people to bring their highest selves to work and self-actualize there. That's what they expected. That's what you promised. Follow through, deliver—or else you will lose these good people. Either they check out or they leave. It doesn't matter. You lose the genius and revert to the routine. And this means achieving your vision isn't possible because you can't do so without the full commitment of your people. Only when VUCA is replaced by Liberating Structures, open communication, and authentic trust can your culture be transformed. When the environment, architecture, and cause are in sync, that's when your people and business thrive.

We Are Energy

When Professor Albert Einstein shared his simple yet elegant equation $E = mc^2$ (energy equals mass times the speed of light squared), it shook the very foundation of scientific thinking about the relationship between matter and energy. Up until his equation was unveiled, matter and energy were seen as separate and unrelated. But, as physicist Dr. Michio Kaku explained in an interview with AwesomeStories.com, "Einstein was able to show that there is a symmetry between energy and matter. And think about it, matter is something we can touch. Our bodies are made out of matter. We can taste matter. We can smell it. But energy is much more nebulous, much more diffuse. And the genius of Einstein was that he was able to show that they really are two aspects of the same thing."

What Einstein really showed us is that we are energy. A single human being is a bundle of seven octillion atoms. It's such a large number it's hard for our brains to grasp. And inside every single one of those atoms is vast energy. Unfortunately, most of us only tap into a fraction of the internal energy at our disposal. Perhaps this is why only one percent of humanity ever experiences self-actualization. That number could be much higher with focused effort. Imagine what we could achieve if we unleashed more of our individual and collective energy.

And remember that all of our internal energy is completely neutral. We can use it in the name of creation or destruction. Both are necessary for growth and evolution. One need only look at human history to see the implications of the choices we make in this regard. How we channel our energy—both individually and collectively—depends on our thoughts and behaviors, which are driven by our hearts and minds. Successful leaders understand this truth.

To ignite and channel the energy of a human system toward alignment, self-actualization, and emergent behavior in the name of an organization's values and noble cause, a leader must inspire, build trust with, and support the hearts and minds of the individuals in their human system. This allows every individual to experience self-actualization. This is how transformative change happens and sustainable high performance and hypergrowth are achieved.

But reaching our full potential as individuals and organizations isn't a destination; it's a journey. It's about overcoming our own limitations in order to help others overcome theirs. It's about creating Liberating Structures that empower individuals to work through challenges together in a trusting, caring, and collaborative environment. All of this takes patience, courage, and determination. Sometimes, we must slow down in order to speed up. Take the time to get your own leadership house in order so that you can create an environment where others can self-actualize and align around something that offers purpose and meaning, a noble cause supported by strong values. This must be able to happen as a result of working for your organization, not despite it. As a leader, this is where you must focus all of your energy. This is the number-one priority of a CEO at a high-performance organization. Tap into the individual and collective energy of the human system that is your organization and amazing things will happen. Ignite the human spirit at work from the inside out, one person at a time. That is the simple, elegant equation of success.

Be "Above the Line"

Business partners Ann Betz and Ursula Pottinga co-founded BEabove Leadership in 2003. Their mission is to provide personal, group, and organizational transformation through coaching, neuroscience, and their trademarked "7 Levels of Effectiveness." I have undergone extensive training with these talented women, who teach organizations how to move from what they call "below the line" energy characterized by hopelessness, fear, and frustration to "above the line" energy, where a high-performing culture can begin to emerge. When people trust that leadership's commitment is long term and that a healthy new employee experience has become reliable and consistent, an "above the line" mindset begins to shape the behavior of the organization's human system. People start to dwell first in a state of courage, then engagement, then innovation, and sometimes achieve synchronicity—also known as emergence. Let's take a closer look at each of these four levels:

Level 4: Courage

When people find courage, they are trusting in the possibility of a positive future—often despite current evidence that a positive future is not likely or predictable. They feel brave and resolute. They describe themselves as happy 55 to 60 percent of the time, which is significantly higher than reported feelings of happiness and productivity below the line. The brain stops succumbing to "amygdala hijacks" and starts to "tend and befriend" rather than fight or flight. This response, which is associated with a release of oxytocin, promotes seeking connections as a response to stress. Connection with others also promotes the release of more oxytocin. Because courage is just above the line, it tends to

be a somewhat unstable level. There is still suscep-
tibility here to the lower-level reactions as well. In
courage, people have the capacity to be physically
aware of how hopeless, scary, or annoying life can
be. The hallmark of this level is the phrase "feel the
fear and do it anyway." There is increasing awareness and willingness to be conscious of and present
with these sensations. What does this mean for your
organization? Well, you're starting to tap into your
human system's potential. People are at least willing
to take a chance and give things a try. In order to
keep an organization's energy above the line, every
small victory and accomplishment needs to be cel-
ebrated. People need to know that their courageous
acts are sought and appreciated. It is unfortunately
all too common that an organization genuinely
moves into a state of courage, addressing ineffective
ways of doing business or communicating, only to
have someone become frustrated, afraid, or hopeless and drag everyone else down. Thus, a good
analogy for this level is keeping a beginning mountain climber on a short and supportive rope as they
attempt a new move. For a leader, this isn't about
controlling things but rather providing very close
and intentional support to the group or organization. This is the stage where the collective begins to
believe in the possibility of a positive future—often
despite evidence that a positive future is attainable.
It is crucial in this stage that distrust is addressed
and steps are taken to restore and rebuild trust. It
is the team's belief and trust in the leader and the
cause that make this level so inspiring and powerful. This is what Steve Zaffron refers to as creating
the future in chapter seven. Trust is key in the state

of courage because all people have is belief in the promise. Actions will be observed and interpreted, and, in the absence of communication, people make stuff up, so it's in this level that frequent and even redundant communication is required to reinforce the truth.

Level 5: Engagement

Engagement is the desire to bring value, to be a contributor. There's basic enjoyment of the work. People are focusing on assets and strengths rather than limitations and detriments. They feel more motivated and tolerant and rate themselves as happy, productive, and fulfilled 68 to 71 percent of the time. In this level, the brain's hemispheres are becoming more integrated. People are further developing their ability to think about what they feel and feel about what they're thinking. They're becoming more capable of inhibiting below-the-line impulses from both their right (freedom) and left (structure) brain hemispheres. The above-the-line aspects of each hemisphere begin to be present, but people aren't yet enjoying all the benefits of using both hemispheres in harmony. Checking in with the body to develop heightened awareness and discernment of bodily reactions is a highly effective strategy for this level. The physical experience of joy and delight as fullness in the heart and a general lightness manifest in positive behaviors and energy. People describe a sense of buoyancy and a spring in their step at this level. When an organization is truly in engagement, so much is possible. Meetings are productive, people help one another, and there is a sense of participation. People want to get ahead but not at the expense of others. Working with an organization at this level is fun and creates what author Ken Blanchard calls "raving fans." Everything of a positive nature works here, from strategic planning and team building to process improvement—you name it. To move the organization or group to an even higher level means boldly and courageously addressing frustrations and an increase in focus on shared vision. An authentic commitment to seeking out and valuing all voices, encouraging mistakes for the sake of learning and growth, and a focus on the individual *and* the whole are keys to moving people to higher levels of happiness, joy, fulfillment, and collaboration, which, in turn, results in higher levels of organizational innovation.

Level 6: Innovation

When the majority of people in your organization start to set aside their egos, personal agendas, and perceived restrictions and explore possibilities from all angles, you've most likely entered the innovation level. Here people are questing for, seeking, and focusing on the most effective solution to the problem or goal. They feel objective and open to ideas and one another. Overall, they report feeling happy, productive, and fulfilled 79 percent of the time. People exhibit an increased ability to engage the prefrontal cortex and calm down their limbic response. There is less of a gap between an automatic stress response and the ability to think and make thoughtful decisions. The brain hemispheres are becoming progressively more integrated, but the left is still somewhat more "in charge" than the right. Rationality and reason prevail. At this level, people start becoming aware that their bodies are predominantly calm. They also start becoming more and more conscious of the fact that their bodily sensations aren't good or bad, just simply informational. The ability to confront challenges from a physiologically calm and centered place is more and more possible. Although many organizations would like to think of themselves as at this level, few truly are. The process of letting go of ego (which is the hallmark of this level) must start from the top. If leaders are still driven to prove themselves, to win and get credit for success, this will stand in the way of true innovation. In an innovative organization, the parts and roles are solidly differentiated but also linked. An organization or group that is truly at this level will have a flat or matrixed organizational chart, because work no longer looks like climbing the ladder. People are playing their appropriate role—one that fits their expertise, passion, and ability. Authentic trust is being built and continuously fortified. When breakdowns in trust occur, as they inevitably will, Liberating Structures are in place to dismantle the VUCA and rebuild trust. At this level, the CEO or president of the organization understands that they have a critical role to play in building trust every day, and so does everyone else. In this phase, people hold themselves responsible for the success of the venture, so top-down management isn't needed and will often feel stifling. Any restrictions will kill creativity, risk taking, and innovation. If you want a culture and an energy of innovation, freedom and exploration are key and will always reap huge rewards when cultivated.

Level 7: Synchronicity

Working from a true understanding that what is within creates what is outside is a hallmark of synchronicity. The focus is on creating a positive experience for all and seeing the gifts and possibilities in everything. Synchronicity is the realm of "magical coincidence." People feel love and experience a sense of harmony. In this level, people report being happy and fulfilled 89 to 100 percent of the time, which is amazing! At this level, the gap between stress responses and the ability to think and make thoughtful decisions is less and less noticeable to oneself and others. The brain hemispheres are very integrated, and the right hemisphere has moved to the default "in charge" position. Focus on holistic thinking and interconnectedness prevails. The body is mostly calm and nonreactive. Everyone's hearts feel full, and people are exquisitely aware of any changes in their energy. They are grounded and present—and have the ability to ground others. Organizations operating at this level are very rare, because the world we live in isn't constructed for this. The structures that seem necessary for an organization of any size are often counterproductive to synchronicity. Even rules, contracts, and written agreements aren't needed because synchronicity is about trust and love. People experience joy and know nothing external is needed. You might ask how groups here get anything done—out of passion, joy, intuition, and the continuing exploration of what will bring joy. Energy moves, and everyone follows.

The benefits of above-the-line culture can't be overestimated. The higher up the levels of effectiveness an organization goes, the stronger their foundation for success. The concepts of each level may sound simple. Helping an entire organization break through to the next level isn't an easy task. It takes a planned, coordinated effort and a big commitment of time and energy. That being said, each breakthrough brings positive change, which translates into more growth, more innovation, more collaboration, and higher performance. Remember, a high-performance culture is a journey, not a destination . . . so buckle up and enjoy the ride.

KEY TAKEAWAYS

- The doorway to culture begins with hiring. Your company must be attracting and recruiting the right people—those aligned with your mission, vision, and values. Top employees look for meaningful work at purposeful companies.

- Infuse your people strategy with strong cultural elements that reflect your organization's noble cause and core values. Build the "why" into this experience and connect to the hearts and heads of your people.

- When the organization's noble cause and values are integrated into every step of the employee experience, alignment, achievement, and self-actualization take center stage. Even performance is measured and rewarded differently. The question isn't whether the manager running the team is good or not. Instead the question becomes whether the manager believes in the organizations noble cause and is fully committed to its mission and vision, and is aligned with its core values and operating in alignment with the agreed-upon thematic goals, priorities, and area of accountability.

- Entanglement and VUCA cause gridlock. This limits growth and makes it extremely challenging to keep pace with marketplace changes without completely burning out your organization. Watch for signs of VUCA and stop it in its tracks.

BRAINHACK

Having a clear understanding of your role as a leader and what's important to you will aid in your efforts to set appropriate boundaries and create a "safe" environment for your brain. Having a clearly defined framework for the culture you want as well as a clear understanding of targets and goals help your brain (and everyone else's) predict more accurate and consistent patterns, which will decrease cognitive scattering and make you less stressed and therefore more productive. At the end of every workday, set aside five minutes and commit to writing a few objectives for the next day. This way, when you wake up in the morning, you have clear goals and a set starting point. Your brain will know what to expect and be able to predict things more accurately, and your day will be significantly more productive.

POWERFUL QUESTIONS

- What is resonating for you in this chapter?
- The doorway of culture begins at hiring. Are you leading this process, or is it leading you? What's the impact on you as a leader and on leadership overall?
- What are you seeing as the signs of gridlock in your team or organization? What's needed from you now?
- What level of effectiveness are you experiencing after this chapter? What are you avoiding? What are you embracing?

CHAPTER 15

Nurturing Humanistic Organizations to Achieve at Warp Speed

"To embrace humanism is to embrace the concept that caring for our fellow human beings is our highest calling."

——SEAN FAIRCLOTH——

I t might seem counterintuitive, but, when you slow down, progress actually speeds up. It's a truth I've seen play out over and over when organizations commit to doing the right things to ignite their culture one human spirit at a time. If your people are still relying on an adrenaline bias to get things done at the speed of light, that means no one is steering the ship. There's no roadmap, no plan. You might have needed that kind of adrenaline rush in your early days as a startup, but, soon after, it actually becomes a problem.

I once worked with a very creative CEO who was guiding his people through a major transition. He sent three hundred of his people to 10 small-group, deep alignment immersion retreats. I'll never forget what he said to me afterwards: "Magi, if we just slow down and have a plan, we can get there faster." The wisdom of his words has always stuck with me. No one likes problems. Everyone just wants them to go away quickly, so we jump in without a plan. This never works. It's always an inefficient use of our precious time. Yet, this is how the vast majority of companies work—reactively, not proactively. This CEO decided to take the necessary time, and the results were strong. His company experienced massive break-throughs in performance. Communication flowed more smoothly. Production numbers were the highest they had been in a decade. Departments that had previously spent time arguing were now collaborating and solving long-term systemic issues as a team.

Throughout the pages of this book, I have encouraged you to prioritize the ongoing journey of personal and cultural transformation—to be intentional and mindful about the changes you want to see in your organization. To do this, you must consciously connect yourself and your people to the big picture—the organization's noble cause, the why, the mission, vision, and values that will take you and your people where you want to go together. This means operating at your highest level and expecting your executive team to do the same. Nurturing your human system and the culture that supports it is where you need to be investing at least 25 percent of your time as a CEO. This is the essence of visionary, transformative leadership. As a reminder, this journey takes grit, determination, and time. Your people will need to be frequently reminded of where the organization is headed and why it matters. It is the leadership team's responsibility to connect people to purpose and shape a self-actualizing culture.

Entrenched and habituated counterproductive behaviors, systemic distrust, and entanglement between people and departments cause expensive reoccurring and systemic problems. If you slow down and plan for change, you're doing the right thing. You see, when you take the time to clear out the VUCA and replace it with a compelling noble cause, concise and focused thematic goals, clear priorities, and smart, well-thought-out architecture utilizing Liberating Structures, you're making room for a better culture and heightened performance. You're getting rid of inefficiencies that cost your organization time, energy, and money. These inefficiencies are holding back your people and hindering growth. When you create a stellar employee-experience strategy that focuses on your organization's values, diversity, and inclusion, you're transforming your hiring and onboarding experience, you're engaging and empowering your people so they can problem solve and collaborate independently, and in turn you're developing and retaining your top talent. As the head of a company, is there anything more important than this? *This* is your job because *this* is what leads to high performance, innovation, and organizational achievement at warp speed. Slow down to speed up. Stop, listen, learn, and reset. This is the secret to success.

WARP SPEED: MARKET LEADER	STATUS QUO: MARKET TRAILERS
☑ Purpose-driven	☒ Ego driven
☑ Self-aware	☒ Excuses and complaints
☑ Response-Agile	☒ Self-preservation
☑ Role Autonomy & Authority	☒ Manipulative
☑ Emotionally Intelligent	☒ Bias for adrenaline, past and mediocrity
☑ Uses healthy and intelligent communication	☒ Unhealthy communication patterns

The foundation of high performance is a strong, healthy culture. The foundation of a strong, healthy culture is trust. As Russian playwright Anton Chekhov once famously said, "You must trust and believe in people or life becomes impossible." Daily life at too many of America's corporations has become impossible. Employees don't trust their bosses, and bosses don't trust them. It's an untenable situation that causes complete gridlock. An *Inc.* magazine article by Lolly Daskal called "30 Quotes on Trust That Will Make You Think," said it best: "Trust is built and maintained by many small actions over time. Trust is not a matter of technique, tricks, or tools but of character. We are trusted because of our way of being, not because of our polished exteriors or our expertly crafted communications." Trust can't be built overnight. It takes time. It lives in authentic conversations, shared daily experiences, and is aligned with words.

Building trust is an ongoing, inside-out job. The first step is to learn to trust yourself. Self-awareness is key. Before trying to help others in your organization, master your own mindset. Be open to continuous self-discovery, personal growth, and change. Being an effective leader of a human system isn't about regretting the past or worrying about the future. It's about learning from your mistakes, bringing your highest self to work each day, being fully present, and planning for a future of healthy high performance and growth. Count on setbacks. They're to be expected. If you're doing the job right, you're becoming a better human and leader every day. Remember, success isn't a destination; it's a journey.

Individual and organizational discipline are required for intentional, sustainable cultural transformation. After individual discipline is achieved, you can help your leadership team become better humans and leaders. All the individuals on this team are invited to do the same personal work you've done. People trust leaders who lead by example, and, since you're walking your talk, you'll earn their trust. As the members of your team learn to trust themselves, they'll also learn to trust others. Lacking courage, some might leave. That's okay. As CEO, you need a team that's ready to roll up its sleeves. Working to continuously improve yourselves together, you and your leadership team can now craft a noble cause and strong organizational values. As a team, you'll embody a courageous new way of thinking and being at work. From this position of strength, trust, and alignment, you and your leadership team can take your message of hope and growth to the whole of your organization. You are ready.

Toward the end of *The Earned Life*, Marshall Goldsmith thanks his friend and 100 Coaches member Carol Kauffman for teaching him a very important lesson:

If I could only have on index card to carry with me for the rest of my life so I could look at it any time of day as a reminder of how I should behave to achieve an earned life, this would be the message I would write on it:

Am I being the person I want to be right now?

Do this once with an affirmative answer and you'll discover that you have earned the moment. Do this habitually and continually and you will create a string of many earned moments, stretching from days into months into years, that add up to an earned life

Goldsmith closes his book, which I highly recommend to everyone, with this poignant idea: "In the end, an earned life doesn't include a trophy ceremony or permit an extended victory lap. The reward of living an earned life is being engaged in the process of constantly earning such a life."

Show your people what *this* looks like every day, and you will show them a better future. Support them on the journey. Shepherd them through the ups and downs. Connect with them as fellow humans. Inspire them through your words and actions. As everyone continues growing, the entire organization benefits. With focused effort, training, and practice, entrenched workplace behaviors and systemic breakdowns are disentangled. Everyone begins self-actualizing as they contribute to the success of the whole human system with a shared noble cause and values. This makes all the difference.

"Trust each other again and again," wrote David Armistead. "When the trust level gets high enough, people transcend apparent limits, discovering new and awesome abilities of which they were previously unaware." This is when emergent behaviors appear, and it is exactly why slowing things down to build trust and eliminate

VUCA actually speeds things up. Trust is a catalyst that, at its highest level, ignites synchronicity and emergent behavior. This, in turn, unleashes exponential growth. Breakthroughs and high performance become the norm. Exceptional organizations arise when everyone is working, growing, and thriving together, aligned around a noble purpose and shared values. Ignite your culture—one person at a time from the inside out—and watch in true awe as the exponential energy of human potential unleashes its wonder.

KEY TAKEAWAYS

- If you slow down and have a plan, you can achieve high performance more quickly.
- Take the time to transform yourself, your executive team, and your culture. Do the work that is required. The investment comes back tenfold.
- Trust is a catalyst that, at its highest level, ignites synchronicity and emergent behavior, which, in turn, unleashes exponential human potential.

BRAINHACK

Of all the brain hacks in this book, the most important is this one. Each day, write down three things you're grateful for. Schedule this into your day. Commit to it. Studies prove that getting into the habit of practicing gratitude can completely change your outlook on life. The more you strengthen the positive neural pathways in your brain, the more active they will become. The best way to get out of despair, hopelessness, fear, and frustration is to find something you're grateful for—even if it's just the coffee that you drink on your way to work or the sound your keyboard makes when you click it. The smallest things make the biggest difference.

POWERFUL QUESTIONS

- What is resonating for you in this chapter?
- What are some recurring and/or systemic problems occurring in your organization?
- What would be possible if these problems were solved?
- What are you grateful for?

If you want to take your learning journey to the next level, I have created a series of trainings that support you in, deepening your learning while equipping you in getting into action to cultivate the kind of culture required to be a market leader.

CONCLUSION

I n September 2022, as I prepared to publish this book, Yvon Chouinard, the founder of Patagonia, made a big announcement: He had decided to give away his company. David Gelles, who writes about the intersection of climate and the corporate world and has covered Patagonia for nearly a decade, reported the event in a September 14, 2022, article in the *New York Times* entitled "Billionaire No More: Patagonia Founder Gives Away the Company":

> A half century after founding the outdoor apparel maker Patagonia, Yvon Chouinard, the eccentric rock climber who became a reluctant billionaire with his unconventional spin on capitalism, has given the company away.

> Rather than selling the company or taking it public, Mr. Chouinard, his wife and two adult children have transferred their ownership of Patagonia, valued at about $3 billion, to a specially designed trust and a nonprofit organization. They were created to preserve the company's independence and ensure that all of its profits—some $100 million a year— are used to combat climate change and protect undeveloped land around the globe.

> The unusual move comes at a moment of growing scrutiny for billionaires and corporations, whose rhetoric about making the world a better place is often overshadowed by their contributions to the very problems they claim to want to solve. At the same time, Mr. Chouinard's relinquishment of the family fortune is in keeping with his longstanding disregard for business norms, and his lifelong love for the environment.
>
> . . . Patagonia will continue to operate as a private, for-profit corporation based in Ventura, Calif., selling more than $1 billion worth of jackets, hats and ski pants each year.

Chouinard told Gelles, "Now I could die tomorrow, and the company is going to continue doing the right thing for the next 50 years, and I don't have to be around."

I was drinking my morning coffee as I read this article and thought to myself, *Now THAT is living in alignment with your purpose and values.* Patagonia, which is one of the elite American companies to generate more than $1 billion in annual revenue, will now live on as a healthy human system fulfilling its noble cause and functioning in alignment with its strong corporate values. I would bet money that there will be no mass departures from the company. In fact, the employees are probably celebrating the news because they share Chouinard's strong commitment to the environment. They also understand that the company must remain competitive and profitable in order to fulfill their founder's plan to have Patagonia's profits funneled into the fight against climate change. The organization's noble cause will undoubtedly unite them, as it has for decades, and inspire the members of this high-performance human system to focus their talent and energy on the goal of helping Patagonia deliver on this important promise.

Companies that understand and value their people prioritize the continuous journey of personal and organizational improvement. The leaders of these high-performance companies are intentional in their efforts to ignite the human spirit at work and nurture the human system that is the life force of their company. They commit to their own personal growth, communicate clearly and authentically, honor their agreements, respect and trust their people, take ownership, and help their people tackle inertia, resistance, and disconnection within their organization. They also unite everyone around their organization's noble cause and values. All of this ongoing attention on organizational culture creates an environment where individuals can self-actualize in collaboration with others, which leads to emergent behavior. Chouinard and Patagonia's path is certainly not for every leader or company, but it clearly demonstrates the exponential, world-changing energy unlocked when people are allowed to thrive and contribute as part of a healthy emergent culture.

REFERENCES

Achor S. (2010). The happiness advantage: the seven principles of positive psychology that fuel success and performance at work (1st ed.). Broadway Books.

Arbinger Institute. (2018). Leadership and self-deception (Third). Berrett-Koehler.

Blanchard, K.H., Bowles, S.M., & Mackay, H. (1993). Raving Fans: A Revolutionary Approach To Customer Service.

Bob. (2021, March 16). *Sensory Acuity: Discover Why Your Success Depends On It.* Life Potential Developments. https://lifepotential.ca/sensory-acuity-wonders/

Britannica, T. Editors of Encyclopaedia (2022, September 3). *Atlas. Encyclopedia Britannica.* https://www.britannica.com/topic/Atlas-Greek-mythology.

Cox, S. A. (n.d.). Diversity and Inclusion – the employee life cycle. *Steven AJ Cox.* https://www.stevenajcox.com/diversity-and-inclusion-employee-lifecycle/

Dweck, C. S. (2006). Mindset: The new psychology of success. Random House.

Eckhart Tolle., Eckhart Tolle|AUTHOR., & Eckhart Tolle|READER. (2015). Transcending the Ego: Finding Our Roots in Being. Eckhart Teachings, Inc.

Edelman Trust Barometer 2022: What you need to know. (2022, May 20). World Economic Forum. https://www.weforum.org/agenda/2022/01/edelman-trust-barometer-2022-report/

Gaton, E. (2021, August 27). *Employee burnout is a problem with the company, not the person.* Harvard Business Review. https://hbr.org/2017/04/employee-burnout-is-a-problem-with-the-company-not-the-person

Goebel, C.J. (2019, June). Newton's laws of motion. *AccessScience.* https://doi.org/10.1036/1097-8542.451410. https://www.accessscience.c om/cont ent/article/a451410.

Herbold R. J. (2004). The fiefdom syndrome: the turf battles that undermine careers and companies--and how to overcome them. Currency Doubleday. http://site.ebrary.com/id/10101454.

Kaku, O. B. M. (2011, December 23). *Michio Kaku's Top 10 Science Stories of 2011.* ABC News. https://abcnews.go.com/Technology/top-10-science-stories-2011-dr-michio-kaku/story?id=15215939

Lencioni, Patrick, 1965. (1998). The five temptations of a CEO: a leadership fable. San Francisco: Jossey-Bass.

Lifecycle Page. (2020, August 10). Adizes Institute Worldwide. https://site.adizes.com/lifecycle/

Luxury Hotels & Resorts: The Ritz. Carlton. (n.d.). https://www.ritz-carlton.com/en/about/gold-standards

Maslow, A. H. (1962). *Toward a psychology of being. Princeton*, N.J., Van Nostrand. Chouinard, Y. (2006). *Let my people go surfing: the education of a reluctant businessman.* New York, Penguin.

Michael F. Broom, P. D. (2021, June 12). *The secret sauce for making teams work.* Center for Human Systems. https://chumans.com/2020/11/18/the-secret-sauce-for-making-teams-work/

Nadella, S. (2017). Hit Refresh: The Quest to Rediscover Microsoft's Soul and Imagine a Better Future for Everyone.

NLP World. (2012, April 11). NLP Sensory Acuity | NLP Glossary. https://www.nlpworld.co.uk/ nlp-glossary/s/sensory-acuity/

Robbins, A. (1997). Unlimited power: the new science of personal achievement (1st Firesideed.). Simon & Schuster.

Rohr, R. (2013). *Falling upward: A spirituality for the two halves of life.* SPCK.

Rosenberg M. B. (2003). Nonviolent communication: a language of life (2nd ed.). PuddleDancer Press.

Strauss, K. (2017, July 26). *How Volkswagen rallied its employees after its emissions scandal (at least for now)*. Forbes. https://www.forbes. com/sites/karstenstrauss/2017/07/26/how-volkswagen-rallied-its-employees-after-its-emissions-scandal-at-least-for-now/

Swiney, J. M., & Aaron Shmookler. (2022, November 21). *About*. The Yes Works. https://www.theyesworks.com/the-team/

The Neuroscience of Trust. (2021, August 31). Harvard Business Review. https://hbr.org/20 17/01/the-neuroscience-of-trust

Tony, T. (2019, April 24). *What is Business Mastery? The 7 Forces of Business Mastery*. tonyrobbins.com. https://www.tonyrobbins. com/career-business/succeed-now-and-in-any-economy-the-7-forces-of-business-mastery/.

Wai, M. K. (2011). The Invisible Lid. *Project Management*. https:// www.projectmanagement.co   m/blog/blogPostingView. cfm?blogPostingID=3693&thisPageURL=/blog-post/3693/ The-Invisible-Lid#_=_

Whitfield, M. (2022, April 6). Why trust has to be at the centre of everything we do. 7 Miles a Minute. https://7milesaminute. com/why-trust-has-to-be-at-the-centre-of-everything-we-do

Wickman G. (2012). Traction: Get a grip on your business. BenBella Books. https://search.ebscohost.com/login.aspx?direct=true&-scope=site&db=nlebk&db=nlabk&AN=477372.

Willmore, J., & Condon, R. (n.d.). The Autonomy Course. https:// autonomycourse.com/

Zaffron, S., & Logan, D. (2011). *The Three Laws of Performance* (1st ed.). Wiley. https://www.perlego.com/book/1006865/the-three-laws-of-performance-rewriting-the-future-of-your-organization-and-your-life-pdf (Original work published 2011).

ACKNOWLEDGMENTS

I am very lucky to have been supported by many family members, friends, and colleagues during the writing of this book. Thank you! Specifically, I would like to thank my mother Rose Battaglia for teaching me about compassion, empathy, grit, and determination. My father Bill Graziano showed me the value of having a strong work ethic and taking initiative. And my sons David, James, and Zachary continue to teach me important life lessons every day. To my grandchildren Sophia, Grayson, Zion, and Chase, you inspire me! You are the future.

Professionally, I would like to thank my first boss, Patricia Whitney, for giving me a chance and teaching me how to make my own way in the world of work. I also owe a big thank you to Marshall Goldsmith for being a pioneer in the field of human development, leadership optimization, and organizational culture. His work has enriched my personal and professional life. I would also like to acknowledge the team at Human Synergistics for providing exceptional ideal/actual-culture data as well as world-class training on how to transform organizational culture. To Ann Betz and Ursula Potting of Be Above Leadership, I am grateful for their groundbreaking research in the area of leadership and neuroscience as well as for creating the seven levels of individual, group, and organizational effectiveness. I am in also debt to the Coaches Training Institute (CTI), which has provided me with powerful training and leadership development as well as the CoActive Coaching and Leadership

Model. Michael Broom deserves thanks for the important training and development he has provided in the area of change management. I am constantly impressed by his lifelong commitment to helping organizations and their people work better together. Finally, I'd like to thank Jeff Wilmore of The Autonomy Course for his dedication to helping people be triumphant.

On my team, a special thanks goes to Jenny Vonnegut for her work on the Brain Hacks found at the end of each chapter. To Lauren Monack and Darlene Huff, I am grateful for your collaboration on the Powerful Questions at the end of each chapter. The entire team at KeenAlignment has played an important supportive role throughout the writing of this book.

Finally, to all the visionary leaders out there who are willing to do the courageous individual and group work necessary to create a strong foundation for sustainable organizational change and breakthrough performance, I commend you. I wrote *Ignite Culture* to support you on your journey.

Made in the USA
Middletown, DE
13 July 2024

57254030R00133